NEW ZEALAND

Food Wine
&Art

NEW ZEALAND

Food Wine &Art

PHOTOGRAPHY: IAN BAKER
TEXT: JEANETTE COOK

CHANEL

Acknowledgements

New Zealand Food, Wine & Art was conceived by the publisher, photographer and the team of people who worked on the book, some of whom worked on our previous bestseller, *Simply New Zealand*.

Ian Baker has again provided stunning and inspirational photographs of the recipes and scenery as well as the many and varied artworks. Thanks, Ian. We trust you enjoyed the food and wine tasting behind the scenes!

Our thanks to the chefs and restaurants, lodges and wineries who have supplied recipes and information, and to all artists and agents who have given their permission to reproduce the artworks in this book.
A list of the artists and galleries who provided assistance in photographing and obtaining works can be found on page 194. Special thanks are due to Judith Dods and Carol Hunter of Kura Contemporary Ethnic Art, Taupo.

There are many talented people who helped put the book together. In no particular order are: the text writer and art advisor, Jeanette Cook; production manager, Barbara Nielsen; designer, Lesley Coomer; the editorial team, Susan Story, Alison Dench, Brian O'Flaherty and Diana Harris; and researchers, Pat Digby and Michelle Hutchinson. I am also grateful for the inspiration of Joan Mackenzie and friends.

To you all a sincere thank you.

Cliff Josephs

All photographs are by Ian Baker except for pages 114, 158, Kevin Judd Photography; and page 94, Fotopacific, Auckland.
Special thanks to our sponsor Agfa-Gevaert NZ Ltd, who supplied all film and processing for Ian Baker.

Photographs on preliminary pages: endpapers, Hunters Vineyard, Blenheim; half title page, Höglund Glass; title page, entering the Tory Channel, Marlborough Sounds; introduction, Mapua Nature Smoke, Mapua Estuary.

Chanel Publishers Ltd
8 Binnacle Rise, Gulf Harbour
P.O. Box 403, Whangaparaoa

First published by Chanel Publishers Ltd, 2000
Copyright © Photography: Ian Baker and contributors as listed above
Text: Chanel Publishers Ltd
Recipes: Remain with the contributing restaurants

Publisher: Cliff Josephs
Photographer: Ian Baker and other contributors
Text writer and art advisor: Jeanette Cook
Production manager: Barbara Nielsen
Recipe editing and research: Susan Story
Design and layout: Lesley Coomer
Editorial team: Alison Dench, Diana Harris, Brian O'Flaherty
Research: Pat Digby, Michelle Hutchinson
Printed by: Midas Printing (Asia) Ltd

ISBN: 0-958208-40-9

Contents

Introduction

New Zealand has traditionally been an agricultural country, with our exports dominated by meat and dairy products, but the last two decades have seen a great diversity of new produce, from fruit, vegetables and nuts to wine and olive oil. At the same time, there has been a proliferation of excellent restaurants and cafés, and a growing range of new foods available. We have begun to excite the visitor and resident alike with our innovative recipes and superb wines. Together with examples of the creativity of the country's artists, these have formed the basis of our exciting new book.

New Zealand Food, Wine & Art is an exploratory indulgence in the sensory delights of this country. This is New Zealand for the epicurean – a sampling of our culture, natural produce and wines. These raw materials are shaped by our master chefs, winemakers and talented artists and spread before the traveller through the keen and unique vision of photographer Ian Baker.

The chefs have drawn on the best and freshest produce available to create superb dishes. They include fish that we are traditionally famous for like tuna, snapper and hapuku, classic New Zealand lamb and beef, and ostrich and venison. There are mouthwatering mussels, scallops and paua, whitebait, crabs and crayfish, luscious freshwater salmon and even quail and pheasant. Meat and fish are accompanied by local produce such as courgettes and kumara, avocados and capsicums and fresh asparagus. Ingredients from Japan, Italy, India, Morocco and Asian herbs and spices reflect our cosmopolitan population and the influences of foreign flavours, ingredients and methods on our own evolving culinary expression. Desserts include a splendid harvest of strawberries, raspberries, black-berries and blueberries, citrus and kiwifruit and our own classic cheeses.

Good food calls for good wine and many restaurants featured have provided their recommendations, often local, to accompany their dishes. New Zealand's wine industry is surging ahead, with the number of wineries increasing dramatically, and our wines winning medals and admirers on the world stage. The reputation of our white wines is well established, but the likes of zingy, herbaceous sauvignon blancs and juicy, lively chardonnays are now being joined by cabernet sauvignon, pinot noir and merlot-based reds of startling quality.

New Zealand art reflects our unique history, cultures and place in the Pacific. The artists highlighted here are a talented mix of ages and stages – some already have a formidable reputation, others are just beginning. The artworks have been selected to provide a sampling of creativity in traditional and contemporary styles from all over the country. Painting, sculpture, printmaking, pottery, fabric art, jewellery and glass works are represented here.

So welcome to our unique world of delights in tastes and artistry. I'm sure they will satisfy your senses – and your soul.

Cliff Josephs
Publisher

Seafood and Sails

Northland and Auckland

The northern tip of New Zealand reaches out into the South Pacific in a long, narrow finger that begins in South Auckland, passes through Auckland city and its narrow isthmus of dormant and extinct volcanoes, then widens out into a knuckle that encompasses Hokianga in the west and the Bay of Islands in the east, and narrows again as it runs up Ninety Mile Beach to North Cape.

Auckland has the largest Polynesian population of any city in the world and the Pacific ambience of the region features prominently in its artwork. Intricately carved ceremonial waka (canoes) and wharenui (meeting houses) reflect the long-held traditions and the ancestral power of the tangata whenua, the people of the land. Susan Firth's colourful ceramic designs, Tom Burnett's and Pamela Wolfe's sunny Northland beaches, iconic borders of shells, tuatara and Maori rafter patterns, and images of tropical fruit, nikau palms and fish all speak of the nostalgic golden summers of youth and a pride in being part of this multicultural society.

This is a region of hot, humid summers and mild, virtually frost-free winters. Its glorious beaches range in colour from the black of the west coast ironsands to glistening shell-pink and white, and subtropical isles and sheltered harbours provide a year-round playground for sunlovers, anglers and boaties. The cuisine of the region is decidedly Pacific Rim, combining marine produce – from juicy mussels to tasty marlin steaks – with citrus flavours, avocados and tropical fruits.

Though Northland does not have the ideal climate for viticulture, some excellent wines – in particular full-bodied reds and chardonnays – are now being produced by boutique wineries in the region. Some of New Zealand's oldest wineries, many established by eastern European immigrants, had their beginnings in Auckland in the early 1900s; greater Auckland is home to the head offices of such big, commercial wine companies as Montana and Corbans, though much of their wine is produced from grapes grown outside the region. The islands of the Hauraki Gulf, Waiheke and Great Barrier, too, are providing some remarkably high-quality wines.

Auckland is a city of sails and seafood, and at the Viaduct Basin, home of the America's Cup, visitors can have their fill of both. The cosmopolitan flavour of New Zealand's largest metropolis can be enjoyed at the Viaduct's 30 or so restaurants, which may offer a range of European culinary delights served with world-class wines, luscious local seafood with New Zealand chardonnay, or simply a plate of South American tapas and a chilled beer.

Above: Omapere Beach, Hokianga, gouache on paper, by Auckland painter Pamela Wolfe.

Chapter opening page: Waiheke Island in the Hauraki Gulf, looking north towards the Coromandel Peninsula. Only 35 minutes by ferry from downtown Auckland, Waiheke has in recent years undergone something of a real-estate boom. Former city dwellers, drawn by the warm microclimate, sweeping beaches, cafés, art galleries, top-quality local wines and relaxed island atmosphere, have left the city bustle behind and become daily commuters, or retired to live there permanently.

Above and right: Kingfish Lodge, built in 1947 at Kingfish Point in Whangaroa Harbour, is the oldest coastal fishing lodge in New Zealand. Maori fished this harbour for centuries, and in the 1920s the fishing grounds were visited by well-known sportsman and author Zane Grey, in his quest for record-breaking game fish. Today Kingfish Point attracts anglers from all parts of the globe.

Char-grilled Kingfish

with bok choy, pink grapefruit and chive hollandaise

4 x 140g kingfish steaks
12 leaves bok choy or pak choy
2 tablespoons Japanese shoyu
2 tablespoons pickled ginger
2 cloves garlic, crushed
2 tablespoons vegetable oil

Red Capsicum Reduction

4 red capsicums, roughly chopped
3 1/2 tablespoons water
3 tablespoons caster sugar
3 tablespoons white wine vinegar

pink grapefruit and chive-flavoured hollandaise
pink grapefruit segments and chives for garnish

Marinate kingfish and bok choy in the shoyu, pickled ginger and garlic for 2 hours.

For red capsicum reduction, whizz capsicums with water in a blender. Strain through a fine sieve. Stir in sugar and vinegar. Put in a pan and reduce. Allow to cool and chill. Bring to room temperature before serving.

To cook kingfish, remove from marinade and drain. Heat an oiled, ridged grillpan to very hot. Quickly cook kingfish for 3 minutes on each side. Make a criss-cross pattern by rotating the kingfish 90° halfway through cooking time, on each side. Remove from heat and keep warm in a low-temperature oven.

To assemble, heat marinade and blanch bok choy for a few seconds. Arrange a bed of bok choy with a little marinade on a plate. Garnish outer plate with red capsicum reduction and chopped chives. Place kingfish on bok choy, drizzle with hollandaise flavoured with squeezed pink grapefruit juice and chopped chives, and arrange grapefruit segments on top with zest.

Serves 4
Recipe prepared by Vikki Coxhead
KINGFISH LODGE
KINGFISH POINT
WHANGAROA HARBOUR

Above and left: Mangonui Fish Shop perches over the water at Mangonui, a picturesque fishing village in the Far North. Few visitors can resist stopping here to admire the old kauri buildings, craft shops and galleries. Patrons can sit in the fish shop's café enjoying a plate of fish and chips while watching the fishing boats returning from Doubtless Bay with their catch. Mangonui Fish Shop has its own fleet, so the fish is as fresh as it gets.

Below: Vice Grip, oil on canvas, by Auckland painter Dick Frizzell.

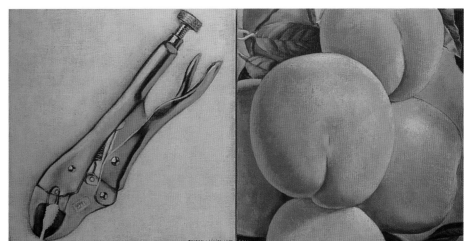

Above: Matapouri Beach, screenprint using water-based paint on French cotton rag paper, by Tom Burnett, Northland.

Left: Kawakawa public toilets, designed by Frederick Hundertwasser. An Austrian-born artist and conservationist, Hundertwasser was invited to New Zealand in 1973 to exhibit at the Auckland Art Gallery, and soon after bought a property near Kawakawa where he lived for most of the last quarter-century. A despiser of the straight line and a lover of colour and fluid form, he designed numerous monuments throughout the world. Hundertwasser died on 19 February 2000, aged 71. This unique public building was completed just days before he died, leaving New Zealand with a lasting memory of his original and creative spirit.

Next page: The Waikokopu Café is close to the Waitangi Treaty House and grounds. The magnificent ceremonial waka in the background is *Nga Toki Mata Whaorua*, named after the vessel in which Kupe discovered Aotearoa. The waka was built in 1940 to celebrate the centennial of the signing of the Treaty of Waitangi. At 35.7 metres long and capable of carrying 150 warriors, including 80 paddlers, it is believed to be the largest waka in existence. The hull was built by Northland tribe members at the inspiration of Princess Te Puea of Waikato, who offered the services of Waikato carvers to decorate the hull. The waka is owned by the five Northland tribes and held in the care of the Waitangi National Trust.

Warm Pumpkin Salad
roast pumpkin, smoked mushrooms
and Puhoi feta

50g manuka woodchips
tinfoil
250g button mushrooms
*1 smallish pumpkin or squash, peeled and cut
into large cubes*
100ml good quality extra virgin olive oil
100g pumpkin kernels
*200g mesclun salad mix (available from
most good supermarkets)*
1 small red onion, thinly sliced
3 tomatoes, quartered
250g Puhoi feta, diced
(you can use any brand of feta)
300g of your favourite salad dressing
(chef has used balsamic)

Place woodchips in a cup made of tinfoil in a frypan. Lay out mushrooms on a wire rack over woodchips. Cover with another pan of equal size or a pot lid, and smoke for 8-10 minutes over a medium heat. Turn off heat and leave covered for another 5 minutes. (Do this in a fish smoker if you have one.)

Once cool, dice mushrooms into large pieces.

Boil pumpkin for 5 minutes or until it is half cooked. Put into an ovenproof dish along with olive oil and pumpkin kernels. Roast in an oven heated to 200°C for 15 minutes or until cooked. After 10 minutes add mushrooms.

In a large bowl toss salad greens, onion, tomatoes and feta together. Add pumpkin, mushrooms, kernels and oil to salad mix. Toss again and divide between four salad bowls. Drizzle with your favourite dressing.

Serves 4

Recipe prepared by
Amanda Turner/Hugh Blues
WAIKOKOPU CAFÉ
WAIKOKOPU

Left: Greenpeace memorial, Matauri Bay, by sculptor Chris Booth. On 10 July 1985, the Greenpeace ship *Rainbow Warrior* was blown up by French government agents while moored in Auckland harbour. Crew member and photographer Fernando Pereira drowned when the vessel sank. The damaged hull was later towed to a spot off the coast at Matauri Bay, north of the Bay of Islands, where it was sunk to become a site for recreational divers.

Marinated Squid
on marinated vegetables

6 squid tubes
4 tablespoons olive oil
4 cloves garlic, crushed
4 tablespoons fresh coriander
2 teaspoons chilli paste
2 kiwifruit, chopped

3 small beetroot
3 carrots
4 silverbeet leaves
50ml each olive oil and lemon juice
25ml balsamic vinegar
1 teaspoon honey
salt and pepper
2 red capsicums, grilled, skinned, deseeded
and puréed
4 char-grilled lemon halves

Cut squid tubes along joins into four pieces
and score on the inside.

Marinate overnight in oil, garlic,
coriander, chilli paste and kiwifruit.

Cut beetroot, carrot and silverbeet into
fine strips and marinate overnight with
olive oil, lemon juice, balsamic vinegar and
honey, plus salt and pepper to taste.

Place marinated vegetables in the centre
of a plate with the red capsicum pureé
surrounding the vegetables.

Char-grill squid so that it curls lengthwise and when cooked place on top of
vegetables. Garnish with halved char-
grilled lemon and red capsicum thinly
sliced.

Serves 4

Recipe prepared by Chris Selby
MARSDEN ESTATE
KERIKERI

Wine: Marsden Estate Pinot Gris 1998

Above: Marsden Estate is a relatively
new winery, opened in September
1997. Some of the grapes used to
make Marsden Estate wines are grown
locally, others are sourced from
Hawke's Bay and Marlborough.
The winery's major output is
chardonnay and cabernet sauvignon,
but it also makes a pinotage, a pinot
gris, a riesling and a muscat.

Opposite, top left: Jump, oil on linen,
by Juliet Bonnay, Whangarei.

Killer Prawn Crazy Crustacean

on rice with a fresh fruit platter

6 slippertail lobsters
6 large scampi
12 mussels
12 large crab claws (or whole crab)
6 large prawns

1 cup long-grain rice

assorted fresh fruit dips, e.g. Thai sweet
chilli sauce, Kikkoman soy sauce, honey
mustard mayonnaise (add honey and hot
mustard to taste)
6 teaspoons each garlic and ginger
juice of ¹/₂ lemon
1–2 tablespoons fish sauce
25g butter
handful chopped coriander

Cut lobster and scampi tails in half, debeard mussels and crack crab claws.

Place all seafood in a draining colander.

For cooking rice, put rice in a heavy-bottomed pot with lid. Place a knob of butter and a little salt in pot and place on heat to brown the rice while stirring continuously. Add enough cold water so that when you touch the rice with your finger, the water comes up to the first joint in your finger. The rice must be flat in pot. Bring to the boil and then turn to low for about 20 minutes with lid on. When rice is cooked, lift up with a wooden spoon. Rice should be light, fluffy and a light brown colour.

While rice is cooking, arrange fresh fruit (preferably tropical, e.g. pineapple, melon, etc) on platter with dips. Heat heavy pan with oil, season seafood, place in pan and flame for a smoky flavour. Place in preheated oven, 220°C, for 8–10 minutes, then put back on stove and add ginger, garlic, lemon juice, fish sauce, butter and coriander. Arrange seafood on rice and pour juice on top, garnish and serve.

Serves 6

Recipe prepared by Owen Sinclair

KILLER PRAWN

WHANGAREI

Opposite and below: Morris & James's café is based at its ceramic factory at Matakana, a little over an hour's drive north of Auckland. Established in 1978 by Anthony Morris and Sue James, the company uses clay dug from the property and today employs 32 clay workers, pot throwers and decorators. In the early 1980s Morris & James was one of the instigators of a new image in commercial pottery, producing planters in bright primary colours where previously most garden pots were glazed in muted, earthy tones. The showroom next to the café displays not only planters, like those seen in the photograph opposite, but also domestic ware, decorative ceramic tiles and wall plaques in tropical Pacific designs, like the one below featuring a nikau palm.

Red Curry Mussels
with crusty bread

2 large onions, peeled and sliced
1 teaspoon ground ginger
4 garlic cloves, crushed
1 tablespoon Thai red curry paste
3 stalks lemon grass, bottom 10cm only, chopped
300ml coconut cream
250ml milk
100ml cream
2 tablespoons tomato purée
48 mussels
1 handful fresh coriander

In a large pot, cook the onions without browning. Add ginger and garlic and cook for 2 minutes. Add red curry paste and cook for 1 minute. Add all other ingredients except mussels and coriander and cook until sauce thickens. Add mussels and poach for 4–5 minutes.

Garnish with fresh coriander and serve with fresh crusty bread.

Serves 4

Recipe prepared by Rob Hume
MORRIS & JAMES
MATAKANA

Pheasant with Red Grapes

poached and seared pheasant and a red grape sauce on courgette ribbons

3 tablespoons olive oil
2 cloves garlic, crushed
1 onion, finely sliced
10 thyme sprigs
200ml white wine
4 cups chicken stock
2 whole pheasants (lightly rubbed with salt)
800g seedless red grapes (4 small bunches reserved for garnish)
2 courgettes (cut into thin ribbons)
½ pumpkin (peeled and roasted)

Cook onion and garlic in olive oil without browning. Add thyme and wine, then reduce and add stock. Bring to the boil, place seasoned pheasants breast-side down in a casserole with a tight-fitting lid and pour hot stock over birds.

Cover and cook for 1 ½ hours at 150°C. (Roast pumpkin in the last 30–45 minutes and the reserved grapes for 10 minutes.)

Blend remaining grapes in a food processor, then bring to boil and reduce by one third. Pass through a fine sieve.

Just before serving, remove pheasant from cooking liquid, cut off breasts and thighs and quickly sear in a pan until golden.

Use pheasant liquor to poach the courgettes for 2 minutes.

Arrange courgettes, pumpkin and pheasant on a pool of warm grape sauce and garnish with reserved grape bunches.

Serves 4

Recipe prepared by Geoffrey Scott
CHEF DE CUISINE
THE HUNTING LODGE RESTAURANT
WAIMAUKU

Wine: Matua Valley Chardonnay 1998

Above: Between September and March the Otakimiro Point headland at the southern end of Muriwai beach west of Auckland becomes the nesting site for more than 1000 pairs of gannets (takapu). These birds begin mating in August and the egg takes 45 days to hatch. By November the whole colony is alive with chicks clamouring for food, while the adult birds – elegant fliers with wingspans of over 2 metres – dive from the cliffs and hit the water at speeds of up 150 kph, returning with food for their noisy young. In February and March, after several weeks of energetic flapping of wings, the young chicks launch themselves off the cliff on their very first flight and, without ever having fed themselves, fly 3000 kilometres directly to Australia. The Takapu Refuge was established in 1979 and the Auckland Regional Council has set up a number of viewing platforms that provide unhindered views of the colony.

Opposite: The Hunting Lodge restaurant is set in a 130-year-old country cottage overlooking the Matua Valley vineyards and winery in Waimauku, 35 minutes' drive northwest of Auckland city. First established in nearby Henderson by the Spence brothers, whose father and grandfather were both winemakers, Matua Valley Wines, one of the larger players in the West Auckland area, produces a range of wines from grapes grown on the home vineyard, and in other parts of the country. Many have won major awards.

Akaroa Salmon
salmon on a fennel slaw with
a tapenade kebab

Fennel Slaw
3 fennel bulbs, washed
juice of ½ lemon
6 tablespoons plain vinaigrette
3 teaspoons chopped parsley

Tapenade Kebabs
6 rosemary sprigs
18 pieces French bread, soaked in 1 cup water
6 tablespoons olive tapenade
12 cherry tomatoes

Sauce
1 cup extra virgin olive oil
3 tablespoons Ponzu (available from
Japanese food stores, a citrus/shoyu combo)
3 tablespoons soy sauce
6 x 200ml fillets Akaroa Salmon
1 sheet nori

To make the slaw, place fennel in salted, boiling water with the lemon juice.

Bring to the boil and simmer until tender. Drain and put into icy water.

Remove when cool, slice finely, add vinaigrette and parsley then season. Serve at room temperature.

To make the kebabs, remove rosemary leaves from the sprig, leaving 2cm on at the end. Skewer soaked bread pieces on the sprig, alternating with cherry tomatoes, then, using a pastry brush, apply all the tapenade evenly on the bread.

To make the sauce, combine all ingredients and store at room temperature. To cook the salmon, remove bones, using tweezers, and skin. Cut six stars out of nori and place on salmon (not the skin side). Season with salt and white pepper. Place on an oiled oven tray with the tapenade kebabs. Bake in a preheated oven, 200°C, until just hot in the centre (5 minutes). Test by inserting a sharp knife into the centre and feeling if it is warm.

Assemble as in photo.

Serves 6

Recipe prepared by Simon Gault
EURO
CENTRAL AUCKLAND

The Auckland Sky Tower, a landmark visible from most parts of greater Auckland, is seen here from Princes Wharf, next to the Viaduct Basin.

Barry Lett's life-sized sculpture *The Fish Lady*, made from riverstones, terracotta brick-stones and mosaic ceramic tiles, stands at the edge of a private garden overlooking Auckland's inner harbour.

Parmigiano Panna Cotta
with balsamic braised figs and
folds of prosciutto

Balsamic Braised Figs
1 cup sugar
2 cups water
1 cup balsamic vinegar
18–24 figs

Parmigiano Reggiano Panna Cotta
240g cauliflower florets (no stems)
40g butter
1 cup cream
60g freshly grated Italian parmesan
1 ½ leaves gelatine

18 slices prosciutto, thinly sliced

To cook the figs, make a syrup with sugar, water and balsamic vinegar.

Simmer for 5 minutes, add figs and place in a deep dish oven tray and braise, covered, for 1 hour at 130°C. Cool and leave in the syrup in the fridge.

Note: Don't use expensive, aged balsamic for this.

To make the panna cotta, put cauliflower and butter in pot and add cold water to come just to top of cauliflower. Simmer for 20 minutes until cauliflower is tender and water has almost evaporated.

Add cream and reduce by half. Add parmesan. Soak gelatine for 5 minutes in cold water.

Puree cauliflower until smooth, then add soaked, drained gelatine. Place in six small, greased moulds and set in fridge overnight or for at least 4 hours.

To serve, layer prosciutto on plate. Demould the panna cotta onto the centre of the prosciutto garnish. Top with a parmesan wafer (optional) and garnish with balsamic figs.

Serves 6

Recipe prepared by David Griffiths and Prue Barton

VINNIES RESTAURANT
HERNE BAY
AUCKLAND

Barbecued Venison

with semolina gnocchi and a sundried
blueberry and macadamia nut salsa

Gnocchi
400ml milk
1 clove crushed garlic
175g semolina flour
salt and freshly ground black pepper

Blueberry and Nut Salsa
180ml fresh orange juice
1 red chilli, chopped
zest of 2 oranges
600g dried blueberries or cranberries
50g brown sugar
50g chopped mint
150g toasted macadamia nuts, chopped

4 x 180g venison (Denver leg)
100ml beef or venison jus, warmed

*Enoki mushrooms and potato shreds to
garnish*

To cook the gnocchi, bring milk and garlic
to the boil. Whisk in semolina flour, salt
and pepper. When thick, cook on a low
heat for 4–5 minutes, stirring occasionally.
Turn out onto a flat tray and spread out
quickly (using a rubber spatula) to 1cm
thickness. Chill.

Stamp out eight rounds about 6.5cm and
pan-fry till golden brown. Keep warm.

To cook the salsa, bring juice, chilli and
zest to the boil, add berries then turn down
the heat and cook for 7–8 minutes. Add
sugar, mint and nuts, mix well, then take off
the heat and keep warm.

Barbecue venison for about 2–3 minutes
and keep warm before serving.

The chef has presented this by placing a
gnocchi round in a cylinder, spooning in
the salsa, pressing slightly to compact, then
removing the cylinder carefully.

Garnish with mushrooms and deep-
fried potato shreds and jus.

Recipe by Paul Edge
IGUACU RESTAURANT
PARNELL, AUCKLAND

Wine : Matua Valley Mathesons
Cabernet/Merlot 1998

The Sky's the Limit, oil on canvas, by
Diana Firth, Auckland.

Decorated earthenware vase and plate, by Susan Firth, Auckland.

Pan-fried Hapuku
with a baked tomato salad and spinach
and potato timbale

Tomato Salad
6 medium tomatoes
50ml extra virgin olive oil
4 shallots, finely chopped
4 sprigs thyme
1 teaspoon crushed garlic
sea salt and freshly ground black pepper
6 Kalamata olives
1 teaspoon sherry vinegar

Potato and Spinach Timbale
6 large potatoes, peeled and chopped
20ml lemon juice
2 teaspoons crushed garlic
100ml extra virgin olive oil
salt and freshly ground black pepper
2 heads spinach, washed

4 hapuku medallions

To cook the tomato salad, cut tomatoes in half and deseed. Place in a single layer on an oiled tray with shallots, thyme and garlic. Season with sea salt and bake in the oven at 150°C until the skin starts peeling from tomatoes (about 5 minutes). Leave to cool after removing skins.

Drain oil from tomatoes and reserve. Roughly chop the tomatoes and olives and place in a bowl with vinegar. Add reserved oil and keep at room temperature.

Boil potatoes until soft, drain well, mash, add lemon juice, garlic and oil and combine. Season and keep warm. Sauté spinach in a little butter, season and just before serving place on top of mashed potato.

To cook the hapuku, sear for 1 minute on each side in a heavy oiled pan. Transfer to a preheated oven, 200°C, for 5–7 minutes.

To assemble, place tomato salad on plates, top with timbale and hapuku. Garnish.

Serves 4

Recipe by Lothar Haberkorn
CAFÉ PACIFIQUE/CARLTON HOTEL
CENTRAL AUCKLAND

**Wine: Kumeu River Brajkovich
Signature Series Kumeu Chardonnay 1999**

Cheeseboard Platter

a selection of New Zealand cheeses served
with seasonal fruit, crostini, olives and feta
as in photo

Antipasto Platter

a selection of piped avocado and salmon
mousse served on crostini with
a cherry tomato

Avocado or Salmon Mousse
1 avocado or ½ fillet salmon
250g cream cheese
125ml sour cream
1 teaspoon sweet chilli sauce
crostini
cherry tomatoes for decoration

Peel avocado or cook salmon fillet and
blend together with cream cheese, sour
cream and sweet chilli sauce to a smooth
consistency.

Spoon into a piping bag and pipe on
crostini. Garnish with tomato.

Serves 6–8

Recipe prepared by Russell Wilson
STONYRIDGE VINEYARD
WAIHEKE ISLAND

Wine : Stonyridge Larose Waiheke
Island Cabernet 1998

Above and opposite: It may look like the Mediterranean, but
this is Stonyridge Vineyard, owned and operated by Steven
White, and it nestles in a sundrenched north-facing valley on
Waiheke Island in the Hauraki Gulf. Since grapes were
planted in 1982 Stonyridge has quickly gained a reputation
for quality – in particular for its prestigious
Stonyridge Larose, which at international tastings has outrated
even reds from Bordeaux. Stonyridge also boasts the oldest
commercial olive grove in New Zealand.

Grilled Chicken Breast

with prosciutto, sage butter, warm potato
and capsicum salad and wilted greens

Potato Salad
400g potatoes, peeled
100g roasted capsicum
25ml white wine vinegar
100ml olive oil
1 teaspoon basil, chopped
Chicken
1 teaspoon sage, chopped
100g butter
1 teaspoon parsley, chopped
2 cloves garlic, crushed
4 chicken breasts
Greens
1 head bok choy, chopped
100g each rocket and spinach
1 tablespoon soy sauce
1 teaspoon sesame seeds
grilled prosciutto and optional bearnaise
sauce to garnish

For potato salad, dice potatoes and cook in boiling salted water until tender, then drain. Meanwhile, process roasted capsicum in a food processor and add vinegar and olive oil. Add this, with basil, to the warm potatoes.

For the chicken, beat together sage, butter, parsley and garlic. Make a pocket along the length of each breast and fill with sage butter. Season with salt and pepper, brush with olive oil and char-grill or pan-fry for about 5 minutes on each side. Finish in oven, 180°C, until cooked (6–8 minutes).

For greens, heat a little oil in a wok and add bok choy, rocket and spinach and toss. Add soy sauce and sesame seeds, tossing until vegetables are wilted but not overcooked.

To serve, place spinach and warm potato salad on warm plates and lay chicken on top. Finish with grilled prosciutto and optional bearnaise sauce.

Serves 4

Recipe prepared by Stephen Thompson
PARTINGTONS/SHERATON HOTEL
CENTRAL AUCKLAND

Wine: Ata Rangi Martinborough Pinot
Noir 1996

The Mudbrick Vineyard and
Restaurant on Waiheke Island is
housed in an old mudbrick building –
the second one built in Auckland in
the last century – and is reminiscent of
a French farmhouse. It has 18 acres
planted in cabernet sauvignon,
cabernet franc, malbec and merlot,
with more recent plantings of
chardonnay grapes. The wine in the
picture is Cabernet Sauvignon/Merlot
1998, described by the owner Nick
Jones as having 'ripe cabernet
characters of green bean, capsicum
and blackcurrants, well weighted
with sweet fruit and firm tannins on
the finish'. Beyond the vineyard can
be seen Rangitoto Island and
Auckland city.

Medallions of Venison
with a kumara and apple rosti,
blackcurrant jus and baby spinach

Blackcurrant Jus
50ml blackcurrant purée
200ml venison jus or substitute with venison
or beef stock

Kumara and Apple Rosti
1 large kumara, grated
½ apple, julienned
1 egg
pinch salt and freshly ground black pepper

Spinach à la Crème
½ onion, diced
200g baby spinach
20g chopped garlic
100ml cream
salt, pepper and nutmeg

360ml venison loin, cut in 4 medallions

To cook the jus, blend ingredients together and reduce for 10 minutes.

To cook the rosti, combine all ingredients. Make small patties and fry in some clarified butter until golden brown. Keep warm.

To cook the spinach, fry onion, spinach and garlic in a little butter. Once spinach is wilted, add cream and seasonings. Reduce and keep warm.

Fry the medallions in very hot olive oil for 2–3 minutes per side. Allow to rest.

To assemble, place rosti on a warm plate, then place a venison medallion on rosti and top with spinach. Spoon jus around. Garnish with wilted strips of capsicum, rosemary and blackberries.

Serves 6

Recipe prepared by Carsten Blutner
MUDBRICK VINEYARD & RESTAURANT
WAIHEKE ISLAND

Wine: Mudbrick Cabernet
Sauvignon/Merlot 1998

Lobster-stuffed Chicken Wings

with cauliflower purée and basil oil

2 fresh, raw lobster tails
1 teaspoon pickled ginger
2 dried shiitake mushrooms, soaked
and diced
sea salt
white pepper
6 tablespoons cream

12 chicken wings, boned

Cauliflower Purée
1 cup chicken stock
$^1/_2$ cup cream
1 cup cauliflower florets
1 teaspoon unsalted butter

1 lemon
6 tablespoons basil oil
2 tablespoons diced tomatoes
6 basil leaves

Cut one lobster tail in half and place half in a food processor with the pickled ginger and shiitake mushrooms.

Season lightly with sea salt and white pepper, whizz for 30 seconds then add the first measure of cream and whizz again.

Dice the other half of the lobster tail and fold through the puréed lobster. Stuff the chicken wings with the lobster, securing the ends of the wings with toothpicks.

Cauliflower Purée
Bring chicken stock to the boil and reduce by half, add second measure of cream and bring back to the boil.

Add cauliflower florets and cook quickly, remove from the heat and strain, reserving cooking liquid. Place hot cauliflower in a blender and add a little of the cooking liquor, whizz briefly and add more cooking liquor, if needed, to make a smooth purée. Put purée back on the stove and add the cold butter.

Stir until incorporated and season to taste. Keep warm until needed.

Roast chicken wings until golden brown,

remove and season. Remove toothpicks and leave wings to rest.

Cut the remaining lobster tail into six medallions and quickly sauté in a little butter. Remove from pan, season and squeeze lemon over lobster. Arrange cauliflower purée on a plate and place two wings and one lobster tail on top of purée.

Drizzle with basil oil and garnish with tomato dice and basil leaves.

Serves 6

Recipe prepared by Dietmar Sawyer
FIVE CITY RD RESTAURANT
CENTRAL AUCKLAND

Wine : Martinborough Vineyard Pinot
Noir 1996

Below: Lapita-Coral, macrocarpa and brass wire, by Virginia King, Auckland.

Above: The dormant volcano of Rangitoto Island in the Hauraki Gulf, viewed from the east Auckland suburb of Mission Bay.

Below: Choice, an etching by Auckland artist Rodney Fumpston.

Saints Eye Fillet
beef with grilled and marinated summer vegetables

4 eye fillet steaks (about 180g each)
2 capsicums, cut in large slices
3 courgettes, sliced
2 tablespoons olive oil
2 tablespoons balsamic vinegar
3 golden kumara
2 tablespoons butter
seasoning
red wine jus (reduced beef stock flavoured with wine)

Clean and trim steaks. Char-grill capsicums and courgettes and marinate in oil and vinegar.

Roast whole kumara, peel and mash with butter and seasoning and a little warm stock if necessary.

Reheat vegetables in the oven and sear steaks on a hot pan to cook.

Deglaze the pan with the red wine jus and serve quickly.

Recipe prepared by Christopher Paul
SAINTS BRASSERIE
ST HELIERS, AUCKLAND

Hot Spots and Cool Wines

Coromandel, Bay of Plenty, and East Cape

The north of this region encompasses the bushclad and beach-studded Coromandel Peninsula, with its giant kauri trees, early goldmining sites and stunning views of the Mercury Islands. Spreading down through lush orchards of kiwifruit, avocados and citrus in the aptly named Bay of Plenty, it passes through the thermal wonderland that surrounds Rotorua and continues around the rugged cliffs of East Cape and the historic beaches of Poverty Bay to Gisborne, ending at the base of Mahia Peninsula.

Gamefishing, hunting and white-baiting are popular pastimes on the Coromandel. This is also 'commune country', and many commune dwellers produce excellent honey and organically grown produce. The Coromandel has over the past 50 years also been home to several well-known painters and artists. Potters Barry Brickell, Helen Mason and Warren Tippett and painters Eric Lee Johnson, Rei Hamon and Michael Smither have all chosen to live there at one time.

Thermal activity is a feature of this entire region – from holes dug in the sand at Hot Water Beach on the Coromandel to the Morere hot springs close to the Mahia Peninsula – but the most vigorous area of activity is in Rotorua where the whole city seems shrouded in steamy mists and bubbling with boiling mud pools. Even the Rotorua Museum and Art Gallery was once a magnificent bath house.

The 11 lakes in the Rotorua district are rich in rainbow and brown trout, many reaching trophy proportions. Rotorua is also a major centre of Maori art and culture, and talented jade and wood carvers continue to develop their work from a traditional base into sophisticated modern designs.

The Bay of Plenty, despite its cornucopia of orchard fruit, is not the best place to grow grapes. But Mills Reef Winery in Tauranga and Morton Estate Winery in Katikati both produce excellent wines, largely from grapes sourced elsewhere.

Further south, though, the vineyards flourish. As signs welcoming you to Gisborne testify, its biggest success story is cool crisp chardonnays, delicious when served with local crayfish. Boutique wineries like The Millton Vineyard now stand up well alongside larger players like Montana and Corbans.

Think of food in this area and picture shellfish – tuatua, pipi, mussels, paua. But food was not always plentiful here. In October 1769 Captain Cook moored the *Endeavour* near what is now Gisborne and sent some of his crew ashore to find supplies. When they came back virtually empty-handed he named the area Poverty Bay, and after skirmishes that left six Maori dead he sailed north around the cape to where pork and kumara were in abundance, anchoring in what he dubbed the Bay of Plenty.

Szechwan Scallops

scallops scented with Szechwan
peppercorns on a fine herb salad
with a wonton basket

Scallops

500g scallops
½ teaspoon each minced garlic, ginger and
lemongrass
20ml sesame oil
30ml olive oil

Garnish

1 packet fresh wonton noodles (available at
Asian supermarket)
100g bamboo shoots (matchstick size)
50g red capsicum, julienned
2 spring onions
50g chervil, Italian coriander, lettuce leaves
(reserve a little chervil to garnish plate)
30g Hijiki seaweed, soaked

To prepare scallops, combine all ingredients in a bowl and leave to marinate.

To cook baskets, mould some of the noodles into two ladles, one on top of the other, and deep-fry in hot oil to create a basket (two per portion).

Sauté scallops in hot pan with a little Szechwan Oil (see recipe following) for 2–3 minutes until medium-rare.

Place 20g of bamboo shoots, 5g julienned red capsicum and a few pieces of spring onion onto scallop to add colour and texture.

Place remaining ingredients in the centre of the plate to create a base for the bottom basket to sit in. Add herb and lettuce mix to bottom of basket, pile scallops on salad and cover with the second basket.

Drizzle Szechwan Oil around plate with the spring onion, a little red capsicum and Hijiki seaweed.

Garnish with remaining chervil.

Serves 4

Recipe prepared by Craig Searle

PUKA PARK

PAUANUI

Szechwan Oil

2 large dried chillies
10g Szechwan peppers
200ml peanut oil
1 fresh large chilli
2 teaspoons minced ginger
2 spring onions, finely chopped

To prepare oil, dry-roast chillies and peppercorns until fragrant. Bring all ingredients to the boil over a low heat, but do not boil. Simmer for 15 minutes and leave to cool.

Chapter opening page: Tall geysers and bubbling hot pools like these seen at Whakarewarewa village near Rotorua have attracted thousands of visitors for more than a century. After Mt Tarawera erupted in 1886 most of the survivors came to Whakarewarewa village to live, next to Pohutu – New Zealand's largest geyser – where they use the abundant thermal waters for bathing, cooking and heating.

Below: This carving by Greg Whakataka Brightwell adorns the prow of a ceremonial waka (canoe) in Rangitukia village, East Cape. The waka was built by the Ngati Porou for the year 2000 millennium celebrations. Ngati Porou is the largest tribe in the East Cape region.

Shell's Marinated Char-grilled Lamb
with Italian vegetable stack

1 cup extra virgin olive oil
1 teaspoon crushed fresh garlic
pinch salt
pinch pepper
dash of lemon juice
500g lamb shortloin
2 carrots
1 yellow courgette
1 green courgette

red wine jus (reduced beef stock flavoured with red wine)

Mix together oil, garlic, salt, pepper and lemon juice. Marinate lamb in this mixture for at least 4 hours (preferably overnight).

Slice vegetables thinly and char-grill. Keep warm in oven. Char-grill lamb until medium-rare. Slice in half. Layer vegetables and top with sliced lamb.

Dish is garnished with capsicum coulis and served with a traditional red wine jus, infused with rosemary.

Serves 2

Recipe prepared by Petra von Allmen
SHELL'S RESTAURANT
TAIRUA

Chilled Avocado Soup

3 ripe avocados
zest of 1 lemon, finely grated
juice of 1 lemon
1 tablespoon honey
1 cup chicken stock
¹/₂ cup cream

Blend together ripe avocados, lemon zest, juice and honey until very smooth.

Add chicken stock and blend again just briefly.

Strain soup into a bowl and stir in cream. Chill well before serving.

To finish, pour over a little avocado oil or pumpkin seed oil and serve with some crisp bread and, as an added extra, caviar.

Serves 4

Recipe prepared by Rick Lowe
SOMERSET COTTAGE
TAURANGA

Mills Reef Winery in Tauranga produces three ranges of wines, all made from Hawke's Bay grapes. Top of the line is their Elspeth range, but the Reserve range also shows the Preston family's excellent winemaking skills. They recommend their Reserve Cabernet/Merlot 1998 as an accompaniment to their restaurant's Cambrian beef dish.

Fillet of Cambrian Beef on Chestnut Mash

with Asian mushrooms, olives and black tiger prawns

400g mashed potato
50g chestnut purée, fresh or canned
4 x 200g trimmed beef fillet
olive oil
12 Kalamata olives, stoned
80g shiitake mushrooms, sliced
12 peeled black tiger prawns
3 cloves garlic, chopped
½ cup red wine
1 cup beef jus
½ cup coriander, chopped

Mix together potato mash and chestnut purée. Keep warm.

Cook beef to required degree and rest for 5 minutes.

Pour a little olive oil in pan, add olives, mushrooms, prawns and garlic.

ite for 2–3 minutes until prawns are 1. Add red wine, reduce by two-thirds. Add beef jus to pan, heat through, add coriander. Spoon a quarter of potato/chestnut purée on to centre of plate, top with beef fillet and arrange prawns, olives and sauce over the top.

Serves 4

Recipe prepared by
Chris Pullin
MILLS REEF WINERY
TAURANGA

Wine: Mills Reef Reserve
Cabernet/Merlot 1998

Moroccan Spiced Lamb

stuffed with basil and gruyère, served on
roasted garlic and kumara mash,
drizzled with balsamic 'Tar'
and chilli oil

Lamb Rumps
4 lamb rumps, trimmed
1 bunch fresh basil
100g gruyère cheese
Moroccan seasoning

Roasted Kumara and Garlic Mash
2 whole heads of garlic
olive oil
salt and freshly ground black pepper
4 large kumara, peeled
1 bunch rosemary

For the lamb, cut a pocket in the lamb
rumps using a sharp knife. Divide basil and
gruyère evenly into four and stuff each
pocket with basil and gruyère.

Sprinkle each rump with Moroccan
seasoning. Preheat oven to 200°C. Seal
each rump in a very hot pan on all sides.

Put rumps into an ovenproof dish and
roast for 10–15 minutes. Take out of oven
and let stand for 5 minutes.

For mash, trim tops off garlic, drizzle
with olive oil and season. Wrap in tinfoil
and bake at 150°C for 15 minutes. Leave to
cool. Dice kumara and boil in salted water
until just cooked. Drain. Finely chop
rosemary leaves.

Squeeze garlic cloves out of their skin.
Add both garlic and rosemary to kumara,
with salt and pepper to taste, and mash.

To assemble, place kumara mash on
centre of plate. Slice rump diagonally and
place on top of mash, then drizzle with tar
and chilli oil (which can be bought at the
supermarket).

Serves 4

Recipe prepared by Peter Flowers
SOLITAIRE LODGE
LAKE TARAWERA

Wine : Trinity Hill Cabernet
Franc/Merlot/Syrah 1997

Balsamic Tar

an economical substitute for aged
balsamic vinegar

2 cups balsamic vinegar

1 1/2 cups sugar

Put vinegar and sugar into a pot. Bring to
the boil then simmer until mixture is
reduced by half and thick and sticky.

Left: Solitaire Lodge is a small, luxury lodge perched on a point that extends into the clear waters of Lake Tarawera. Because this deep lake has a shingle rather than mud bottom, it is reputed to produce the finest tasting trout in the region. Looming over the lake is Mt Tarawera, which erupted violently during the night of 10 June 1886, killing many people and burying several villages in ash. The eruption also destroyed the famous pink and white terraces on nearby Lake Rotomahana.

Below: Aotearoans, carved from macrocarpa by Opotiki sculptor Peter Radley.

Guide Maggie, acrylic on canvas, by June Grant, Rotorua. 'Maggie' Papakura, one of the many guides who used to live in the Whakarewarewa village, was the artist's great-great-grandmother. An entrepreneur and leader of the Tuhourangi people, she was the first Maori woman to gain a BA from Oxford University.

Woodlands Lamb
lamb loin on a capsicum couscous with
plum and rosemary relish and sweet
potato quenelles

1 each potato, carrot, courgette, capsicum
4 kumara
1 teaspoon garlic, crushed
4 x 100g fully trimmed lamb loins

500g plums
½ cup red wine
150g sugar
1 sprig rosemary, finely chopped

1 cup couscous
1 cup chicken stock
¼ teaspoon turmeric
1 eggplant, sliced and pan-fried
fresh rosemary

Parisienne cut vegetables (cut to shape in photo) and leave to one side. Peel, cook and mash kumara. Rub lamb with garlic and pan-fry or char-grill for 7 minutes and leave to rest.

While lamb loin is cooking, reduce whole pitted plums with red wine, rosemary and sugar until plums are pulpy.

Add couscous to boiling chicken stock with turmeric and seasoning. Stir until liquid is absorbed and leave to rest for 3 minutes. Boil prepared vegetables and cook until al dente.

Slice lamb onto couscous and pan-fried eggplant disc. Drizzle plum relish around and evenly scatter baby vegetables and add quenelles of kumara mash. Use fresh rosemary for garnish.

Serves 4

Recipe prepared by Simon Wright
PRINCES GATE HOTEL
ROTORUA

Tomato Bisque and Basil Sorbet

basil infused sorbet with a chilled
tomato bisque

Sorbet
125g fresh basil
175g sugar
1 cup water
¹/₂ cup each dry white wine and champagne

Bisque
5 large ripe tomatoes
1 medium red onion, chopped
1 clove garlic
2 tablespoons tomato paste
¹/₄ teaspoon Kaitaia Fire (chilli sauce)
1¹/₄ cups chicken stock
large sprig basil
salt and freshly ground black pepper

For the sorbet, remove basil leaves from stems, wash and shake dry. Boil sugar and water together for 5 minutes, then cool.

Process basil leaves in food processor with a little of the white wine until you have a fine, pulpy liquid. Mix sugar syrup, remaining wine and champagne, then stir in basil mixture. Pass mixture through a fine sieve or a damp muslin cloth, squeezing to extract as much liquid as possible. Freeze liquid in an ice cream maker according to manufacturer's instructions, or freeze it until mushy, beat in a chilled bowl and freeze again. Do not remove sorbet from freezer until you are ready to serve, because it will soften very quickly.

For the bisque, place all ingredients in a saucepan, cover and cook on low heat until tomatoes and onions are very soft. Process in a food processor then strain through a fine sieve. Chill soup and adjust seasoning. Serve with a scoop of basil sorbet in each bowl, and garnish with deep-fried strips of basil. You could also add a thin line of fresh cream around the sorbet if desired.

Serves 4

Recipe prepared by James Reddington
ACTON LODGE, GISBORNE
Wine: Huntaway Reserve Gisborne
Chardonnay 1998

Smoked Lamb Shanks
lamb with creamed potato and
baby carrots

3 tablespoons flour
6 lamb shanks, lightly smoked
75g clarified butter, divided
2 each onions and carrots, sliced
1 leek, diced
3 sticks celery, sliced
3 cups mushrooms, quartered
2 cloves garlic
1 1/2 cups port or red wine
2 tablespoons tomato paste
1/4 cup plain flour
beef stock
2 bay leaves
1/2 cup baby carrots

creamed potato, to serve

Flour and season shanks. Place in a hot pan with a little of the clarified butter and brown. Set aside.

Heat a medium-sized pot, add a little more clarified butter and sauté all vegetables except baby carrots.

Add port and tomato paste, stir and reduce. Thicken with flour to form a roux. Add lamb shanks and sufficient beef stock to cover shanks well, add bay leaves, cover pot and place in the oven at 180°C for 2–2 1/2 hours.

When cooked remove shanks and keep hot. Skim then sieve remaining sauce into a pot, add baby carrots and simmer until they are cooked.

Finish sauce by stirring in 2 tablespoons of butter.

To serve, place some creamed potato on a plate with lamb shanks alongside and spoon over sauce with some baby carrots.

Garnish with a sprig of Italian parsley.

Serves 6

Recipe prepared by Robin Pierson
BUSHMERE ARMS
GISBORNE

Wine: Millton Te Arai Merlot/
Cabernet 1998

Opposite: The winery at The Millton Vineyard in Manutuke, Gisborne. James and Annie Millton established the property in 1984 and the estate now encompasses four separate vineyards. No insecticide, systemic fungicide or soluble fertilisers are used in the vineyard, making Millton New Zealand's first fully certified organic commercial winegrower.

Chorizo Risotto

capsicums, olives and spicy sausage in a
creamy risotto

Risotto
1 large onion, finely diced
6 cloves garlic, chopped
fresh thyme
100ml olive oil
300g arborio rice
salt and pepper
450ml chicken stock (or water)

4 chorizo sausages
2 roasted red capsicums, julienned
24 black olives
14 smoked garlic cloves
200ml tomato purée
50g butter

cooked green beans
basil oil
balsamic vinegar

Sauté onion, garlic and thyme in oil.

Add arborio rice and seasoning.

Gradually add liquid. Cook until al dente (firm to the bite – about 9 minutes).

Take out of pot and spread on a flat tray. Leave to cool.

Slice sausages and sauté in a large pot. Add remaining ingredients then add risotto and heat through.

Garnish with green beans, basil oil and balsamic vinegar.

In the photo the chef has also used some mushrooms and a red capsicum coulis to garnish.

Serves 4

Recipe prepared by Diane Kirk
CAFÉ VILLAGGIO
GISBORNE

Decorative stoneware pot by Barry Brickell. Barry has lived at Driving Creek in Coromandel for several decades and still carts clay and firewood through his property on his now-legendary miniature train. He and his friends continue to extend the Driving Creek railway, and today many visitors to the area stop by to take a ride.

Volcanoes and Verdant Pastures

Waikato, Central Plateau and Taranaki

Waikato is rich dairy-farming country. It is also the breeding ground of some of the finest racehorses in the world. Travellers through the northern part of this region are treated to green paddocks bounded by crisp, white fences and dotted with shady macrocarpa and oak trees, with willows and poplars edging the streams. Hamilton is the business and supply centre for this agricultural region, and through its centre flows the deep, dark Waikato, New Zealand's longest river and the source of much of the region's healthy pastureland. Southeast of Hamilton is Cambridge, a tidy tree-lined village that looks almost as English as its namesake. Out west through Ngaruawahia towards the coastal towns of Raglan and Kawhia the area becomes more hilly, with steep limes-tone country and unusual rock outcrops. Further south into the King Country are large caves, the most notable being the labyrinth at Waitomo whose giant limestone deposits and millions of glow worms attracted tourists as far back as 1887.

This area is steeped in history, and many of the famous battles of the land wars were fought here. Historic sites include the terraced hilltop defences at Meremere. In Ngaruawahia, seat of the Maori queen, ceremonial canoes are sometimes moored beside the Turangawaewae marae.

The Waikato Museum of Art and History boasts an extensive collection of nineteenth-century works, in particular paintings by von Tempsky and Kinder, and some excellent Maori carving, including the Turangawaewae war canoe *Te Winika.*

South of this region, the central plateau is dominated by Lake Taupo, often referred to as the trout fishing capital of the world, and at its southern end is Turangi, whose rivers also abound with trout. Both these areas also have geothermal pools. The Tongariro National Park is a World Heritage area, and on a clear day the snow-covered volcanic peaks of Ruapehu, Ngauruhoe and Tongariro tower over the landscape. Part of this area was gifted to the people of New Zealand in 1887 by Te Heuheu Tukino IV, paramount chief of the Tuwharetoa people, to protect the tapu (sacredness) of these peaks for all time.

In the southwest of this region is Taranaki with mighty Mt Taranaki as its centrepiece. Art is well represented in this region, too, and much can be seen at the large Govett-Brewster gallery in New Plymouth, including works by New Zealand-born avant-garde artist and filmmaker Len Lye.

The produce from this region is varied and delicious and fine restaurants abound. Lake Taupo's fat trout are legendary, and if you catch one your lodge restaurant will often agree to cook it for you. The Taupo region is also the place to sample venison, wild pork, pheasant and rabbit. Eltham in Taranaki is famous for its cheeses, particularly European-style delicacies such as danbo, havarti, gouda and blue vein.

Ripples, a mixed media work by Christchurch sculptor Neil Dawson, is suspended high above the Waikato River like an enlarged reflection of the concentric ripples in the water below.

Chapter opening page: Mt Ruapehu erupting in 1996. The Ruapehu skifields were closed for two consecutive seasons while the volcano sent out dramatic explosions of ash, steam and rocks.

Below: Whakamaru village, near Mangakino, on the edge of the lake created by a hydroelectric station dam on the Waikato River.

Manuka Baked Salmon

baby salmon with fresh herb polenta
and pesto sauce

Polenta Cake
1 cup water
1 tablespoon oil
1 1/2 cups polenta (fine cornmeal)
1/2 cup fresh herbs, chopped (parsley, chives,
thyme, basil)

Dressing
1 cup fresh basil leaves
1 tablespoon white wine vinegar
1/2 cup oil
seasoning to taste

Salmon
2 baby salmon (700–900g) available from
fish shops or supermarkets
small manuka branches

lime wedges, chives and manuka flowers to
decorate

For polenta, bring water and oil to boil, then simmer. Add polenta and herbs. Mix well. Polenta will go to a thick paste – keep stirring. Turn heat right down and cook for a further 25 minutes. Line a small slice tray with tinfoil and brush with oil. Pack polenta into tray about 1cm thick. Put into fridge to set.

For dressing, blend basil and vinegar together in a blender, add oil and seasoning.

For salmon, place half manuka on baking tray with salmon on top, and remaining manuka on top of this. Season and bake at 200°C for 5–7 minutes.

To serve, cut polenta into triangles and quickly pan-fry to golden brown.

Drizzle sauce around plate and place polenta flat in middle with salmon on top.

Garnish with lime wedges, chives and flowers.

Serves 4

Recipe prepared by Dean Burgess
THE NARROWS LANDING
HAMILTON

Wine: Mills Reef Reserve
Chardonnay 1998

Above: The historic paddleboat MV *Waipa Delta* made its first voyage on the Waikato River in March 1877. It now runs popular cruises that leave from opposite the Hamilton town centre.

Below: Rocks and Sandpool, an original screen print by former Taranaki artist Michael Smither, who now lives on the Coromandel Peninsula.

Char-grilled Beef

eye fillet with roasted garlic and creamy
orzo pasta with smoked mushrooms

4 x 200g beef eye fillet
4 sprigs sage

6 tablespoons sundried tomato pesto
6 tablespoons feta
6 tablespoons ricotta

Orzo Pasta
1 ½ cups orzo pasta
24 smoked button mushrooms
4 sundried capsicums
2 small Spanish onions
4 cloves garlic
1 cup cream
salt and freshly ground black pepper
8 strips of carrots to line moulds

*2 bulbs garlic, halved and roasted in olive
oil, salt and pepper with fresh thyme*

For the pesto topping, combine all
ingredients and reserve.

For the orzo pasta, cook pasta, then
refresh and add rest of ingredients and
reduce a little.

To serve, put pasta mix into round
moulds, lined with carrot, and serve under
beef which has been char-grilled and
topped with pesto. Roasted garlic bulb sits
on top of beef.

The chef serves this with a balsamic and
Moroccan spiced jus and some deep-fried
pepperoni sausage.

Serves 4

Recipe prepared by Harry Williams
TABLES ON THE RIVER
HAMILTON

Lemon Tart
served with berries and vanilla ice cream

500g short pastry

Curd
5 lemons
300g caster sugar
8 eggs
300ml cream

Roll out pastry and line a 23cm tart tin. Chill.

Zest and juice lemons. Stir sugar and eggs together, add lemon juice and zest. Gently stir in cream.

Blind-bake tart base at 180°C for 12 minutes. While hot, pour in curd, turning oven down to 140°C. Cook until jelly-like in centre – approximately 30 minutes.

Cool on rack.

Serve with vanilla ice cream and fresh berries.

Serves 8

Recipe prepared by Mark Hollands
THE GALLERY
CAMBRIDGE

There has been an increasing trend for restaurants to double as galleries, showing works by local artists. The painting shown here in The Gallery restaurant is *Maungakawa Hill*, an oil on canvas by Cambridge artist Rodney Hamel.

Hinengaro, oil pastel on paper, by
Taumarunui-born painter Albert
McCarthy.

Flax 3, a triptych in gesso, acrylic and
oil on board, by Taupo painter
Penny Wilson.

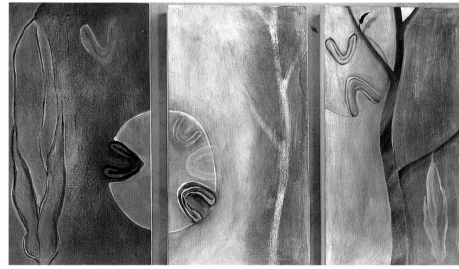

Huka Lodge Cervena

with courgette fritters, mushrooms,
truffled rice and red wine gravy

Grilled Field Mushrooms
6 field mushrooms
2 tablespoons olive oil
salt and freshly ground black pepper
4 tablespoons unsalted butter

Remove stems from mushrooms and
drizzle with olive oil. Season lightly and
dot butter on mushrooms. Grill and bake
slowly until tender.

Courgette Fritters
3 courgettes, coarsely grated
2 teaspoons sea salt
1 egg
2 tablespoons self-raising flour

Salt grated courgette with sea salt and
stand for 1 hour. Add egg and mix well.
  Mix in self-raising flour. Fry small
spoonfuls until golden brown.

Truffled Rice
1 cup long grain rice, well rinsed
1 ½ cups strong chicken stock
2 teaspoons truffle-infused olive oil
1 teaspoon sea salt

Mix rice, stock, oil and salt. Bring to the
boil, whisk well and lower heat to lowest
possible setting. Cover pot and allow to
cook for 15 minutes. Remove from heat and
cool in pot. Cut into shapes, e.g. triangles,
if desired.

Not far from Huka Lodge are the
Huka Falls, where the Waikato River
surges through a narrow chasm to
plunge in a mass of seething, milky
spray surrounded by a fine rainbow.
Further down it settles into a deep
turquoise pool, before again plunging
through a rocky cut to the next pool.
It continues to zigzag through its
dramatic course till it is harnessed by
the Aratiatia power station.

Red Wine Gravy
150ml port
375ml red wine, reduced to 180ml
500ml strong beef stock

Reduce port to 50ml, add reduced red wine. Simmer beef stock until it coats the back of a spoon. Add port and wine mix to stock, boil and keep warm.

1kg Cervena loin

To prepare Cervena, dry loin well and season with black pepper and sea salt. Seal well on all sides and roast at 150°C for 20–25 minutes on a cake rack.

Remove from oven, cover with foil and allow to rest for 10 minutes. Capture juices and add to red wine gravy.

Carve Cervena and serve with garnishes. The chef has added a watercress purée, spinach dumplings and a béarnaise sauce.

Serves 6

Recipe prepared by Nicholas Huffman
HUKA LODGE
TAUPO

Wine: Corbans Cottage Block Cabernet Sauvignon/Franc 1994

Smoked Lamb Rack
manuka-smoked lamb with sweet corn
and tomato salsa

2 lamb racks, cut in half
manuka woodchips for smoking
24 baby sweetcorn spears
6 tomatoes
50ml olive oil
salt
fresh Italian parsley
¼ cup spring onion
3 garlic cloves, finely chopped
chilli oil
chilli to taste

Begin by smoking lamb racks in a smoker or in a frypan with a small handful of manuka chips and lamb placed on a cake rack. Tightly cover with tinfoil, then heat over a low heat until woodchips start smoking. Smoke lamb for 15 minutes.

Char-grill corn spears until char marks appear, then remove from grill.

Pan-sear lamb racks to seal in juices, then place in hot oven on baking paper to finish.

While lamb is cooking, roughly dice tomatoes and roughly chop parsley and spring onion. When lamb is done (approximately 20 minutes), allow to rest in a warm place for 5 minutes.

While lamb is resting, sauté garlic, parsley and tomatoes in olive oil, adding salt to taste, until tomatoes are warmed.

Place sweet corn and tomato salsa in centre of plate with lamb rack on top. Garnish with Italian parsley and chilli oil.

Optional Tuscan Crust
½ cup grated parmesan cheese
1 cup breadcrumbs
1 teaspoon dried Italian herbs

Mix together and place on lamb 5 minutes before lamb is finished cooking.
Serves 4

Recipe prepared by Darren Edge
THE BRANTRY
TAUPO

Wine : Sacred Hill Basket Press
Cabernet Sauvignon/Merlot 1998

Evening light on Lake Taupo. Covering an area of 619 square kilometres, Lake Taupo is one of the largest lakes in the southern hemisphere. This serene expanse of water used by anglers, yachties and waterskiers was not always so benign – it is actually a water-filled volcanic crater created by a violent eruption 22,500 years ago, and has seen 28 lesser eruptions since, the most recent in AD 186.

Pork and Sage Fillet

pork fillet with a sage and onion stuffing,
mushroom risotto and apple jus

2 pork fillets
75g butter
2 onions, diced
2 garlic cloves, crushed
16 sage leaves, chopped
12 pieces fresh bread
1 egg
12 spinach leaves
1 each red, yellow and green capsicums
75g melted butter
200g mushrooms
150g short grain rice
450ml water or chicken stock

jus of reduced stock and diced apples

Cut pork fillets in half lengthwise, then flatten out with a meat mallet.

For the stuffing, melt butter, add 1 onion and garlic and cook without browning. Add sage and crumbled bread, then add egg to bind. Season with salt and pepper.

Put spinach in boiling water for 1 minute, then plunge in iced water. When cold, remove spinach and squeeze water out.

Place flattened pork fillet pieces down, then cover each with a quarter of the stuffing, with 3 spinach leaves over stuffing. Roll pork fillet into roll shape.

Cut capsicums into strips and cook with a little olive oil in oven until just cooked.

Make rice risotto by sweating off remaining diced onion and mushrooms, then add rice, season and cover with water or chicken stock. Cook until all liquid has been absorbed by rice.

While rice is cooking, roast pork rolls in oven at 170°C for 15 minutes.

To serve, place risotto in the centre of plate, cut pork on an angle and garnish with capsicums and jus as illustrated.

Serves 4

Recipe prepared by Wayne Third
GRAND CHATEAU
NATIONAL PARK

Wine: Ata Rangi Martinborough
Célèbre 1996

Above: Pregnancy and Hat, a bronze work by Taupo sculptor Graham J. Cooper. The bronze has been cast by the Artworks Studio foundry using a 'lost wax' process developed by the ancient Egyptians in about 5000 BC.

Left: The Grand Chateau at Tongariro, a landmark on the slopes of Mt Ruapehu, can be seen for miles around. Buses leave from nearby to transport skiers to the Whakapapa skifield. In a good skiing year the snow has been known to cover the ground around the Chateau, and on a few rare occasions intrepid skiers have actually been able to ski off its sloping roof!

Pesto Beef Fillet

eye fillet, root vegetable rosti, beans,
roasted tomatoes and Galaxy blue
cheese wonton

Rosti

1 medium (150g) carrots
1 medium (150g) potato
1 medium (150g) kumara
3 tablespoons olive oil

Wonton

50g Galaxy blue cheese
8 wonton wraps

200g green beans
12 baby tomatoes
4 x 150g beef fillet steaks
4 tablespoons basil pesto

For rosti, grate carrot, potato and kumara.
Squeeze out excess moisture with
paper towel. Mould mixture into four
small cakes and pan-fry in olive oil until
golden brown (allow 3-4 minutes per side).
Allow to cool.

For wonton, place 1 teaspoon blue cheese
in middle of wonton wrapper.

Wash wrapper edges with water and
place another wrap over the top. Seal edges
with firm finger pressure. Deep-fry in
olive oil until golden brown.

Baste green beans and baby tomatoes in
olive oil and roast at 180°C for 5 minutes.

Reheat rosti in oven.

Grill beef steaks for 3–4 minutes on each
side or to the degree required, then rest for
2–3 minutes.

Serve beef on top of rosti and roast
vegetables, add pesto and top with wonton.

Garnish with deep-fried basil leaves.

The chef has also used hollandaise sauce.

Serves 4

Recipe prepared by Christopher Burton
BACKSTAGE CAFÉ
STRATFORD

Mountain House Lodge, on the
slopes of Mt Taranaki. The painting
is an oil on canvas by resident artist
and managing director of the lodge
Keith Anderson.

Pepper-wine Venison
venison steaks, potato pompoms and
pepper-wine sauce

Sauce
6 tablespoons Maggi Brown Gravy Mix
12 chopped mushrooms
6 thinly sliced apple slivers
½ teaspoon cracked peppercorns
12 tablespoons red wine

olive oil
*6 x 150g portions venison fillets or shortloin,
cut into finger-thick steaks*
6 tablespoons redcurrant jelly
*fresh celery leaves and fresh parsley to
garnish*
30 potato pompoms, cooked

For the sauce, mix gravy mix with water
according to packet instructions and bring
to the boil. Add mushrooms, apples,
pepper and wine. Mix well and simmer
until well combined and apples are cooked.

Heat a little olive oil in a solid frypan to
high heat or use a hot grill.

Quickly sear venison steak on both sides
until medium-rare.

Arrange meat on plate, drizzle sauce over
top and garnish with redcurrant jelly and
parsley. Put celery leaves and potato
pompoms around plate.

Serves 6

Recipe prepared by Berta Anderson
MOUNTAIN HOUSE LODGE
STRATFORD

Wine: Collards Cabernet/Merlot 1998

Winelovers' Wonderland

Hawke's Bay and Manawatu

The Ruahine and Tararua ranges run down the centre of this region like a giant backbone, interrupted at the university town of Palmerston North where State Highway 3 cuts through from west to east. On the eastern side of the ranges is Hawke's Bay, the second largest grapegrowing area in the country. On the western side are the pasturelands and hill country of the Manawatu, while the historic Whanganui River meanders down from the north and empties into the sea at Wanganui just below Taranaki.

The flat lands of the Manawatu are dairy country, while on the high-country farms around Taihape, Feilding, Marton and Hunterville rugged sheep clamber up the steep hillsides above the magnificent Rangitikei River.

Manawatu Art Gallery in Palmerston North and the Sarjeant Gallery in Wanganui show work by the many talented artists in this region, including sculptors Paul Dibble and Jeff Thomson, and potter Wi Taepa.

On the other side of the ranges, Hawke's Bay, like the East Cape further north, is rich in seafood and shellfish, and has an abundance of orchard fruit. Dotted around the countryside are many market gardens supplying vegetables to the large canneries in the Hastings area, which is particularly noted for its green asparagus.

But, above all, Hawke's Bay is a winelover's paradise, its climate producing a more diverse range of grape varieties than anywhere else in the country.

Hawke's Bay contains a broad mix of wine producers ranging from large, commercial wine companies such as Vidal Estate and Villa Maria's Esk Valley Estate, to boutique-style family enterprises like Crab Farm Winery. During the 1850s New Zealand's first grapevines were planted here by the French brothers of the Society of St Mary to provide altar wines for the church. Today the Society still owns the winery and the Mission Estate enjoys an excellent reputation. And Te Mata Estate Winery, though given a new image by Wellington architect Ian Athfield, has retained the oldest winery building still in operation in New Zealand.

Napier and neighbouring Hastings are architectural delights, but this visual bounty is the result of a tragic past. A massive earthquake in February 1931 killed 258 people and destroyed most of the towns buildings, which were rebuilt in the style of the time – 1930s art deco. Napier's Marine Parade, edged with tall Norfolk pines, has a marineland and an abundance of English-style resort entertainment, and would have provided homesick pioneers with a little slice of Brighton Beach.

Around Hastings and Havelock North graceful colonial farmhouses, their sweeping driveways lined with English trees, preside over large sheep stations. Many of these holdings have been in the same families for generations. Horse shows are popular with these residents and, true to their English heritage, participants and spectators sport an elegant mix of tweed, cavalry twill and cashmere.

Venison Ragout
with chilli, tomatoes, bratwurst and beans

1 red onion, diced
2 cloves garlic, crushed
2 rashers bacon, sliced
1 bratwurst, sliced
500g tomatoes, diced
1 red capsicum, seeded and diced
1 red chilli, seeded and finely chopped
1 sprig thyme
1 sprig rosemary
½ teaspoon cumin powder
salt and freshly ground black pepper
1 punnet cherry tomatoes
10 green beans, blanched
4 x 100g pieces venison (Denver Leg)
small bunch watercress

Sauté onion, garlic, bacon and bratwurst in a hot wok until onion is softened. Add diced tomatoes, capsicum, chilli and chopped herbs. Cook for 5 minutes, then add cumin and seasoning.

Take off the heat and add cherry tomatoes and green beans.

Sear venison in a hot pan and season well. Roast at 200°C for 8–10 minutes for medium-rare and rest well before serving.

To asemble, place ragout in the centre of the plate and top with a little of the watercress. Slice venison and nestle it into watercress.

Garnished with shaved parmesan and grissini (breadsticks) in the photo.

Serves 4

Recipe by Scott Kennedy
VAVASSEUR
PALMERSTON NORTH

Wine: Saint Clair Rapaura Reserve
Merlot 1998

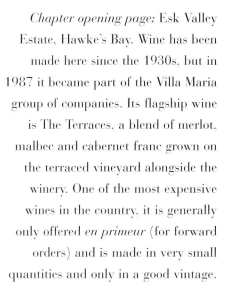

Chapter opening page: Esk Valley Estate, Hawke's Bay. Wine has been made here since the 1930s, but in 1987 it became part of the Villa Maria group of companies. Its flagship wine is The Terraces, a blend of merlot, malbec and cabernet franc grown on the terraced vineyard alongside the winery. One of the most expensive wines in the country, it is generally only offered *en primeur* (for forward orders) and is made in very small quantities and only in a good vintage.

Overleaf: Anatole's café in the County Hotel, formerly the Hawke's Bay County Council offices. These are Napier's oldest reinforced concrete buildings, constructed in 1908 in typical Edwardian style on a corner site. The massive parapets fell off in the 1931 earthquake and were not replaced until it was converted to a boutique hotel in 1994.

Poached Pork Loin

with a compote of dried fruit and a creamy
mustard sauce

Fruit Compote
500g dried fruit (prunes, raisins, etc)
½ cup balsamic vinegar
½ cup brown sugar
¼ cup port

4 pork loins 180g each

Poaching Liquid
2 cups water
1 cup white wine
¼ cup white wine vinegar

Mustard Sauce
1 tablespoon seeded mustard
¼ cup white wine
½ cup thickened cream

Place all the fruit compote ingredients in a medium-sized saucepan and cook carefully, allowing the liquid to reduce by three-quarters or until the fruit sticks together (about 30 minutes).

Meanwhile, preheat a frying pan and brown the pork. While the pork is browning bring the poaching liquid to the boil then place the pork in it to cook through (15–20 minutes).

Just before the pork is cooked, heat the sauce ingredients in a small pan, reducing by half.

To serve, place the compote in the centre of the plate (use a mould to shape if desired), cut the pork on an angle and place around the compote. Drizzle the sauce over the pork and garnish with mint and a strawberry if desired.

Serves 4

Recipe by Wade Durrington
ANATOLES
NAPIER

Wine: Te Mata Coleraine
Cabernet/Merlot 1990

Salmon with Avocado Mousse

pan-seared salmon with rainbow chard,
avocado mousse and a crisp linguini garnish

Mousse
150g cooked broccoli
1 ripe avocado
2 whole eggs
1 egg yolk
50ml cream
60g cream cheese (softened)
seasoning

20g squid ink linguini pasta
100ml olive oil, saving a little to cook the
salmon
4 x 200g salmon steaks

small stalks rainbow chard
or baby spinach, lightly wilted
herb-infused dressing

To make the mousse, preheat the oven to
150°C and place the first seven ingredients
in a food processor.

Blend but do not overmix. Pour into
greased timbales or ramekins and bake
covered in tinfoil in a waterbath for about
30 minutes.

Cook pasta until firm to the bite and
refresh in cold water. Dry well and
shallow-fry in olive oil until crispy, then
dry on paper towel.

Heat a frying pan using a little olive oil
and fry seasoned salmon for 2 minutes on
each side until just cooked. Cover and rest
until needed.

To assemble, reheat the mousses in a
microwave (1½ minutes for 4 serves if
necessary). Serve with salmon, some herb-
infused dressing and fresh chard leaves,
plus coriander or chervil. Spike pasta into
salmon to create height.

Recipe by Kym Fell
MANGAPAPA LODGE
HAWKE'S BAY

Wine: Craggy Range Winery
Chardonnay 1999

Below left: These giant Batocera longhorn beetles crawling over the Manawatu Art Gallery are made of painted bronze. The sculptor is Elizabeth Thomson from Wellington. The works were cast in pieces at Artworks Studio in Auckland using the ancient 'lost wax' method, and returned to the artist to assemble and add detailing, brazing and finishing.

Below: Sculptor Paul Dibble's Pacific Monarch, located in front of the Manawatu Art Gallery and illuminated at night, is a landmark for Palmerston North. It is probably the largest bronze sculpture to be cast in New Zealand. Paul Dibble's work is created at The Foundry, his studio in Palmerston North.

Next page: Founded in 1897 by Tom McDonald, The McDonald Winery in Napier retains his name despite its purchase in 1989 by Montana. It now produces premium wines under the Church Road label. Montana have reconstructed some of the history of European and New Zealand winemaking in a museum housed in what was once an underground vat.

Asian Salmon

with hot/sour sauce, risotto
and Italian vegetables

Italian Vegetables
1 red and 1 yellow capsicum, roasted
4 florets cauliflower, blanched
2 tablespoons balsamic vinegar
4 tablespoons extra virgin olive oil
2 tablespoons coriander, chopped
2 cloves garlic, crushed
Maldon salt and cracked pepper

Risotto
1 red onion, finely chopped
2 tablespoons olive oil
1 cup arborio rice
2 cups salmon or fish stock
2 tablespoons fresh coriander, chopped
2–3 tablespoons pickled ginger, chopped
2 tablespoons butter to finish

Hot/Sour Sauce
1 cup salmon or fish stock
¼ cup oyster sauce
2 fresh chillies, seeded and chopped
2 cloves garlic, chopped
3 kaffir lime leaves, finely chopped
¼ cup lime juice
1 tablespoon olive oil
½ cup basil and coriander, chopped
4 x 150–200g salmon fillets

Marinate capsicum and cauliflower in vinegar, oil and seasonings and set aside.

To cook risotto, sweat onion in the oil till lightly coloured then add rice and stir to toast for a few minutes. Add warm stock gradually until all is absorbed and the rice is creamy but still firm. Add remaining ingredients and serve immediately.

While the rice is cooking, prepare the sauce by combining all ingredients except the chopped herbs and simmering gently. Add herbs and thicken if desired with a teaspoon of arrowroot.

Cook salmon on a char-grill and serve with risotto, vegetables and sauce.

Serves 4

Recipe by Murray Milne
McDonald Winery, Taradale

Wine: Church Road Chardonnay 1998

Top Left: Take 5 restaurant on Napier's Marine Parade is housed in one of the stately Victorian buildings known locally as the Six Sisters. Designed by early Napier architect Charles Lamb and built around 1890, they miraculously escaped the devastation of the 1931 earthquake. Today they are home to restaurants, offices, a bed and breakfast and an art gallery.

Cranberry Lamb
with kumara and sage mash

1kg red kumara
¹/₂ cup purple sage, chopped
2 parsnips
1 lamb rack, no excess fat
¹/₄ cup wholeseed mustard
1 cup dried cranberries
Jus
1 cup beef stock
¹/₂ cup cranberry sauce (or more to taste)
¹/₂ cup red wine

To prepare mash, peel kumara and boil in lightly salted water until soft. Drain well, add sage and keep warm.

Peel parsnips and cut with potato peeler into long strips. Deep-fry or oven bake until crisp and set aside for garnish.

Sear rack in a hot, oiled pan then spoon on mustard and pat on cranberries.

Roast in oven, preheated to 180–200°C, until cooked to desired stage (10 minutes on average, depending on size).

While meat is roasting, combine jus ingredients and warm through.

To assemble, spoon mash onto plates, cut rack in half and link bones. Place on top of mash, drizzle jus over rack and top with parsnips.

Served with carrots and courgettes in the photo.

Serves 4

Recipe by Coralee Kenrick
TAKE 5 WINE & JAZZ BAR
NAPIER
Wine: Linden Estate Reserve Vintage
Cabernet/Merlot 1996

Life-sized corrugated-iron bull by Auckland sculptor Jeff Thomson, currently artist in residence at the Sarjeant Gallery, Wanganui.

Smoked Beef Stack

with marinated mushrooms, salsa verde
and char-grilled vegetables

Salsa Verde
2 cloves garlic
1 teaspoon Dijon mustard
2 anchovies
1 tablespoon capers
1 tablespoon caper juice
1 cup mixed herbs (basil, dill, oregano)
½ cup soya oil

Marinated Mushrooms
2 cloves garlic
2 tablespoons sesame oil
12 button mushrooms
2 tablespoons coriander, chopped
1 tablespoon brown sugar

Char-grilled Vegetables
1 eggplant
3 capsicums (yellow and red)

500g scaloppini
*400g smoked beef (Scotch fillet, roasted to
medium-rare if smoking unsuitable)*

To prepare the salsa verde, purée all the
ingredients except oil in a blender. Add oil
slowly until the salsa has emulsified.

To prepare mushrooms, sauté garlic in
sesame oil for 1 minute, add mushrooms
and remaining ingredients and cook until
mushrooms soften.

To prepare char-grilled vegetables, slice
eggplant and capsicum into 10-cm strips.
Blanch scaloppini in boiling water, and cut
in half. Put all vegetables into a bowl,
season and oil well, then char-grill on both
sides for 2–3 minutes.

To assemble, place vegetables on the
plate, slice beef and arrange on top, then
drizzle with salsa verde and garnish with
mushrooms. Chives and purple basil can
be added too.

Serves 4

Recipe by John Voice
VIDAL ESTATE RESTAURANT, HASTINGS

Wine: Vidal Estate Cabernet
Sauvignon/Merlot 1998

Opposite top right: Palm trees and a carillon in Clive Square, Napier. The bells of
the carillon are electronically operated to play tunes every half hour. Clive Square
was laid out in Victorian style at the turn of the century. A few days after the
1931 earthquake temporary shops and offices were erected here and for a short
while the square became a tiny town.

Right: The Heritage Fountain (Nga Puna Wai Whakapapa), a steel assemblage by Napier sculptor Paratene Matchitt, was constructed in front of the information centre on Marine Parade, Napier, in 1996. In his work Matchitt combines images from both Maori and Western cultures, and creatively explores the European religious images that were developed as icons of Te Kooti's Ringatu church – the six-pointed star, a bleeding heart pierced with an arrow, a triangle and a cross.

Green-leaf Scallops

with saffron tagliatelle, olive tapenade and zucchini purée

¼ teaspoon powdered saffron (2 packets)
40ml pernod
20ml olive oil
180g whole eggs (approximately 3)
325g strong white flour (high grade)
1½ teaspoons salt
50ml toasted sesame oil to dress pasta

Chive Oil
1 bunch chives, blanched and refreshed
100ml extra virgin olive oil

8 generous spinach leaves, blanched and refreshed
24 scallops, roe on
50ml toasted sesame oil to brush scallops
4 teaspoons tapenade

To make pasta, soak saffron in the pernod for 10 minutes, add olive oil and the eggs. Process flour and salt in a processor, then add the egg mixture with the machine running until a ball forms. Rest, covered, for 1 hour, then shape into tagliatelle using a pasta machine. Cook in boiling salted water for a few minutes until al dente, then drain and toss in sesame oil. Roll into four bundles and reserve.

Purée the blanched chives with the extra virgin olive oil, strain and reserve.

Lay blanched spinach leaves out in pairs and arrange 6 scallops on each. Season and roll tightly into sausage shapes. Brush a tray and the scallops with the second measure of sesame oil and roast at 190°C for 5 minutes.

Place a piped circle of Zucchini Purée (see recipe following) and a teaspoon of tapenade on each plate. Arrange pasta and scallops (cut in half lengthwise) and drizzle chive oil around.

The chef serves this with a deep-fried tomato skin and a drop of mushroom oil.

Serves 4–6

Recipe by Vicki Bruns-Bolderson
RD1 RESTAURANT, HASTINGS

Wine: Sileni Estates Chardonnay 1998

Zucchini Purée

1 zucchini
40ml olive oil
1 clove garlic
verjus (made from unfermented, unripe
grapes, available at good delicatessens)
salt and freshly ground black pepper

Purée the zucchini with the oil, garlic and enough verjus to make a thick purée. Season to taste and reserve.

Left: RD1 is the restaurant on the Sileni Estates, one of Hawke's Bay's newest wineries. The winery, covering 110 acres in two separate regions, produces chardonnay, sémillon, merlot and cabernet.

Below: *After Five*, acrylic on paper, by Jane Gray, Havelock North.

Venison Liver

liver and bacon in a creamy mustard sauce
with a stuffed baked apple

Stuffed Apples
4 apples
1 medium onion, chopped
1 tablespoon sugar
¹/₂ teaspoon cinnamon
2 tablespoon raisins

Liver and Bacon
500g venison liver
(ox or calf liver can be used)
salt
50g butter
100g bacon, chopped
2 tablespoons wholegrain mustard
50ml cream

Cut the tops off the apples and reserve. Scoop out the apple flesh with a melon baller and reserve. Discard the core. Process the apple flesh and onion in a blender with the sugar and cinnamon for a short time. Add the raisins and mix with a spoon. Fill the apples with this mixture and replace the tops. Place the apples in an oven dish, add a little water then cover tightly with tinfoil and bake in oven, 200°C, for approximately 15 minutes.

To cook the liver, clean the liver, cut it into thick slices and season with salt. Heat the butter in a frying pan and place the liver on one side and the bacon on the other (or use another pan for the bacon). Sear liver quickly, then turn over. Add the mustard and cream. Don't overcook the liver.

To serve, place the apple on the plate and arrange the liver and bacon. Stir the remaining sauce and pour over the liver.

Serves 4 as an entrée

*Recipe from Kees Peters
and Joss Lamers*
CRAB FARM WINERY
NAPIER

Wine: Crab Farm Pinot Noir 1995

Left: Crab Farm's vineyard restaurant. The painting is by local artist Stu Duval. Crab Farm Winery is on reclaimed land that belonged to winemaker Hamish Jardine's great-grandfather. Until the 1931 Hawke's Bay earthquake lifted it above sea level, it was covered with tidal water and was home to hundreds of crabs. The vineyard now covers 12 acres and produces pinot noir, cabernet, chardonnay and sauvignon blanc.

Below: Pikopiko, a hand-built, unglazed pot by Wanganui ceramic artist Wi Taepa.

Beehives and Boutique Wineries

Wairarapa and Wellington

North of Wellington, over the steep Rimutaka Range, lies the fertile Wairarapa valley. Every weekend Wellingtonians make the trip over the winding hill road, or take the somewhat straighter route by train, to buy fresh fruit and vegetables from orchards and market gardens, honey direct from the beekeepers and above all to go on a tasting tour around the wineries. After all that tippling a return car journey is out of the question, so country cottages, farmstays and lodges have sprung up to cater for the Wellingtonian overnighter, and Martinborough now has cafés and restaurants that are as sophisticated as any in the capital.

Back in 1844 the country's first sheep stations were established around Martinborough. This was then a quiet backwater, and quite recently Martinborough was described by the *Evening Post* as 'a picturesque and drowsy country town on the road to nowhere'. But in 1979 it was pointed out that its climate and soils were very similar to the Burgundy region in central France, and since then there has been a gradual spread of boutique vineyards in the Wairarapa. Today there are some 35 wine producers in the valley, including larger concerns like Palliser Estate Winery, Martinborough Vineyard and Ata Rangi Winery.

Martinborough is definitely going somewhere. Epicureans flock from all over the country to the Martinborough wine, food and music festival, keen to sample award-winning pinot noirs, venison and lamb, fresh asparagus, salmon and whitebait from the rivers that flow out to the sea on the rugged eastern coast, and delicious honey from orchard beehives.

On the other side of the Rimutakas, Wellington has a beehive of a different sort. This is the centre of government, and the CBD is dominated by the parliamentary Beehive and its older surrounding buildings, many of which date back to early settlement. The city is often referred to as the 'cultural capital' of New Zealand. Everywhere you look there are public sculptures and galleries, from Civic Square and the City Gallery to the waterfront promenade and the new and controversial Te Papa museum and art gallery. Wellington's biennial month-long festival of performing and visual arts has become legendary, and top international and local events are booked out well in advance.

Dining out in the capital is often a formal affair, an opportunity to dress elegantly and sample dishes by some of the country's top chefs in surroundings as sophisticated as any in Paris or New York. Wellington may have a reputation as a windy city, but the air is clear and fresh, and in cafés and restaurants the conversation is as sharp and sparkling as the city's harbour. And along the historic Kapiti Coast, once the battleground of the great warrior Te Rauparaha, the warm climate and long beaches at Paraparaumu and Waikanae attract hordes of weekend sunbathers and swimmers.

Stuffed Quail

Italian sausage-stuffed quail served with a
pinenut pilaf

1 onion, finely chopped
2 tablespoons butter
300g Italian sausage (any Italian-type
sausage that is not heavy in garlic,
skins removed)
16 fresh sage leaves, finely chopped
1 tablespoon parsley, chopped
freshly ground black pepper
4 quail (rib cage removed)
4 large rashers streaky bacon
50g clarified butter

Sauté onion until soft in a little butter.
Mix onion, sausage, sage and parsley.
Season with freshly ground black pepper.
(The sausage should have enough salt – to
check seasoning, fry a small amount, taste
and adjust seasoning and herbs if
necessary.)

Lay quail on a board and divide stuffing
between them (about 70ml per bird).

Reshape quail, secure with toothpicks
and tie legs together with oven bag ties,
then wrap neatly in bacon. Place in
roasting dish with clarified butter, and
roast for 20–30 minutes at 220°C. Remove
and rest in a warm place for 10 minutes,
covered with foil. Remove toothpicks
and ties.

Make a pan sauce with the juices, or a
plum vinaigrette – equal quantities of
traditional plum sauce, boiling stock (or
water) and olive oil.

Serve on pinenut pilaf or couscous with a
green vegetable.

Serves 4

Recipe prepared by Lois Peter
AYLSTONE
MARTINBOROUGH

Wine: Muirlea Rise Pinot Noir 1996

Chapter opening page: Wellington's
Parliament Buildings, House of
Representatives and the Beehive.

Above: Palliser Estate Winery
produced its first wines as recently as
1989, but through the talents of
winemaker Allan Johnson, who gained
his skills at the prestigious Roseworthy
College in South Australia, it has
become one of the Wairarapa's leading
stars. More than half its output is now
exported to eight different countries.
Palliser has built its international
reputation on its white wines, but its
outstanding pinot noir has also won
several awards.

Right: Palliser Estate has consistently
won awards for its Martinborough
Sauvignon Blanc. Its trophy collection
includes several prestigious Air New
Zealand National Wine Show awards,
one of which is shown here.

Seared Scallops
with leek purée and pickled walnuts

450g leeks, sliced (trimmed weight)
10g butter
70g crème fraîche
120ml fish stock
2 tablespoons walnut oil
20g butter
3 tablespoons olive oil
42 scallops
150g pickled walnuts (5–6 slices per person)
6 walnut halves (lightly toasted)

Cook leeks in first measure of butter with a lid on until soft. Purée in blender until smooth.

Fold in crème fraîche and season. Place in a saucepan and reheat when required.

For the sauce, gently heat stock and walnut oil until warm. Take off the heat and whisk in second measure of butter.

Heat a pan until very hot, add olive oil and immediately cook scallops.

Place purée in centre of plate and drizzle sauce over. Place scallops and pickled walnuts around plate and garnish with a walnut half.

Serves 6

Recipe prepared by Steven Harris
WHAREKAUHAU LODGE
PALLISER BAY

Wine: Martinborough Vineyard
Wharekauhau Chardonnay 1998

Wairarapa Lamb

a rack of lamb with tapenade crust,
mushrooms and roasted vine tomatoes

200g olive tapenade
6 lamb racks
½ cup polenta
½ cup fresh herbs (e.g. marjoram, thyme, chives)
2–3 cloves garlic, or to taste
6 large, flat mushrooms
6 trusses vine tomatoes

Mint chutney or redcurrant jelly

Press tapenade over fleshy part of lamb racks and roll in polenta. Chop herbs and garlic and sprinkle over mushrooms. Place mushrooms and tomatoes in a lightly oiled baking dish, and roast in preheated oven, 200°C, for about 20 minutes until cooked. Remove from oven and keep warm. For medium-cooked lamb racks, roast for 10 minutes, then turn off oven and rest for a further 8 minutes. Cut each rack in half and serve on a mushroom, accompanied by a truss of roasted tomatoes. Serve with mint chutney or redcurrant jelly.

Serves 6

Recipe prepared by Nicky Brindle
TOADS LANDING
MASTERTON

Wine: Solstone Wairarapa Valley Merlot 1996

These mythical birds, made of glazed
and fired clay, are by ceramic artist
Nicky Brindle, the owner of Toads
Landing restaurant.

This barracuda sculpture by Wellington architect John Grey adorns Napier sculptor Paratene Matchitt's bridge, a walkway that spans Jervois Quay and leads to the maritime park and Te Papa on Wellington's city waterfront.

Snapper with Crab Mash

snapper, basil and crab mash, roasted tomato sauce and spinach ravioli

Roasted Tomato Sauce
1 tablespoon olive oil
10 oven-roasted tomato halves
3 shallots, quartered
3 cloves garlic, quartered
1 chilli pepper, seeded and chopped
2 sprigs thyme
2 ½ cups chicken stock
½ cup plus 3 tablespoons soft butter
1 teaspoon lemon juice
salt and black pepper

Spinach Ravioli
6 leaves of spinach
olive oil
4 wonton wrappers

Crab Mash
120g crab meat
200g mashed potato
6 leaves fresh basil, chopped
extra virgin olive oil
600g fresh snapper (or similar)

For the roasted tomato sauce, heat oil in a sauté pan. Sauté tomatoes, shallots, garlic and chilli. Add thyme then simmer for 5 minutes. Add stock and cook for 10 minutes or until reduced by half. Purée until smooth. Strain through a fine sieve. Return to pan. Whisk in butter, lemon juice and seasonings. Keep warm.

For the spinach ravioli, sauté spinach with a little olive oil. Season and purée. Place a teaspoon of cooled purée on a wonton wrapper and shape into ravioli. Cook ravioli in salted boiling water.

For the mash, add crab meat to hot mashed potato and fold in chopped basil.

For the snapper, heat olive oil in a hot pan. Sear on both sides until just cooked.

Pour sauce onto plates, place fish on top and garnish with ravioli, mash and basil.

Serves 4

Recipe prepared by Chris Green
Boulcott St Bistro, Wellington
Wine: Alana Estate Martinborough
Chardonnay 1998

Paua Fritters
with avocado and wasabi salsa

1 cup self-raising flour
1 teaspoon baking powder
3 eggs
250ml milk
1kg paua (abalone), minced
100g red onion, diced
3 tablespoons coriander, chopped
75ml sweet chilli sauce
50ml lime or lemon juice
salt and freshly ground black pepper
oil for cooking

Avocado and Wasabi Salsa
1 ripe but firm avocado
1 large lime, juiced
1 tablespoon finely chopped red onion
2 tablespoons good quality olive oil
2 teaspoons coriander, finely chopped
1 ½ teaspoons prepared wasabi
salt and freshly ground black pepper to taste

For the fritters, sieve flour and baking powder into a bowl and make a well in the centre. Lightly whisk eggs and pour with the milk into the well and whisk together. Fold all other ingredients into batter mix.

Preheat a non-stick pan or barbecue to medium heat and lightly oil. Cook a small amount to taste and correct seasoning before cooking fritters.

For the salsa, dice avocado into 1cm cubes and combine with remaining ingredients. Carefully fold together, trying not to mash avocado. More wasabi can be added, depending on personal taste.

Serves 4–6

Recipe prepared by Steve Logan
LOGAN BROWN
WELLINGTON

Wine: Martinborough Vineyard
Sauvignon Blanc 1999

Above: Memento Mori, lithograph by
Gavin Chilcott, Wellington.

Below: Remnants of a Wedding Landscape,
mixed media on canvas, by Wellington painter
Sally Reweti-Gould.

Above: Povi 2000, lithograph by
Michael Tuffery, Wellington.

Waikanae Crab Cakes
crab and salmon risotto cakes with herb
mayonnaise and mixed lettuce salad

*2 tablespoons olive oil
1 small red onion, finely chopped
300g arborio rice
850ml fish stock
100g salmon fillet, cut into 2cm cubes
450g Waikanae crab, well drained
1 egg, lightly beaten
3 tablespoons olive oil for frying*

To make risotto, heat olive oil in pan, add
red onion and cook until softened.

Add arborio rice and stir well to coat
grains. Have stock heated in a separate pot
and gradually add as needed to risotto –
this will take about 15 minutes.

Add salmon and stir through gently
until salmon is just cooked. Remove from
heat and leave until cooled. Add Waikanae
crab and beaten egg and mix well.

Shape mixture into 12 cakes and chill
overnight.

Heat olive oil in pan and cook cakes for
about 5 minutes on each side until nicely
browned.

Serve with homemade herb mayonnaise
and mixed lettuce salad.

Serves 6

Recipe prepared by David Nichol
BUBBLES BISTRO
PARAPARAUMU

Wine: Vidals The Bays Chardonnay 1996

Below: St Pauls Anglican Cathedral in
Wellington was designed by
Cecil Wood in 1935, but, possibly
because of financial restraints during
the Depression, building did not
commence until 1954, when
HM Queen Elizabeth II laid the
foundation stone during a royal visit.
Built in four stages, the church was not
completed until 1998.

Crab and Seafood Risotto

with mussels, scampi, salmon and fresh herbs

Risotto

1 small onion, peeled and diced
4 cloves garlic, finely chopped
1 1/2 tablespoons olive oil
1 tablespoon butter
6 sundried tomatoes, sliced
1/2 cup arborio rice
2–3 cups fish stock infused with lemon
250g crab meat

16 fresh mussels
4 crab claws
12 fresh scampi
2–3 tablespoons olive oil
1/2 cup fish stock
1/4 cup white wine
chopped basil, parsley and chives
200g diced salmon and groper

Cook onion and garlic in oil and butter until they are just translucent. Add sliced sundried tomatoes and arborio rice. Sauté for 2–3 minutes, stirring continuously. Add stock, little by little, until rice is half cooked (about 10 minutes). Add crab meat and continue adding small amounts of fish stock until risotto is slightly al dente, yet creamy.

Heat a pan on high heat, add mussels, crab claws, scampi and olive oil and deglaze with fish stock and white wine. Simmer for 2–3 minutes with lid on pan, add half the fresh herbs and set aside.

Add diced salmon, groper and rest of fresh herbs to risotto and fold through so fish is just cooked.

Spoon risotto onto each plate and garnish with sautéed seafood and herbs.

Serves 4

Recipe prepared by
Mark Hartstonge and Jason Roberts
DOCKSIDE RESTAURANT
AND BAR
CENTRAL WELLINGTON

Above: One of several metal nikau palms that are a predominant feature alongside the public library building in Wellington's Civic Square. The palms were created by Wellington architect Ian Athfield.

Opposite: Wellington's Dockside Restaurant on Queens Wharf looks out over the harbour and the overseas terminal building.

Passionfruit Soufflé
served with vanilla ice cream

6 eggs
sugar to coat moulds
3 tablespoons butter
3 tablespoons flour
³/₄ cup milk
¹/₄ cup passionfruit pulp
¹/₂ cup sugar
1 teaspoon vanilla essence
pinch salt

Separate eggs. Grease and sugar six medium-sized individual soufflé moulds.

Melt butter in a pot, add flour, whisk until well blended. Slowly stir in milk.

Cook, stirring, until mix is almost boiling and is thick and smooth.

Add passionfruit and sugar; cook for 2 minutes. Remove from heat, add vanilla and cool slightly.

Add 4 egg yolks, one at a time, beating to incorporate each one before adding the next. Add a pinch of salt to 6 egg whites and beat to a soft peak. Stir a quarter of the egg white into sauce, then carefully fold in the rest.

Pour into moulds and place in middle of preheated oven, 180°C. Bake the soufflés for 15–20 minutes until they are risen and tops are brown. Serve with vanilla ice cream.

Serves 6

Recipe prepared by Paul Hoather
THE WHITE HOUSE RESTAURANT
ORIENTAL BAY
WELLINGTON

The White House is one of the many cafés and restaurants overlooking Wellington's Oriental Bay, a favourite spot for joggers and city workers taking a lunchtime break.

Owen Mapp's nephrite jade and tourmaline waka pendant on a gold base hangs from Hanne Eriksen Mapp's braided sterling-silver chain.

Marinated Raw Tuna
with a capsicum and tomato garnish

500g fresh tuna
70ml virgin olive oil
70ml red wine vinegar
½ teaspoon whole black peppercorns
½ teaspoon coriander seeds, crushed
3 sprigs fennel fronds
3 sprigs basil, finely chopped
½ teaspoon sugar
3 whole garlic cloves, peeled and chopped
1 medium red onion, finely diced
1 whole red capsicum, finely diced
1 stalk celery, finely diced
1 whole tomato, peeled, seeded and diced
sea salt and freshly ground black pepper

Cut all the tuna into 2cm x 7cm x 0.5cm-thick slices and place in a deep dish or bowl.

Whisk together oil, vinegar, peppercorns, coriander, fennel, basil, sugar and garlic. Add remaining ingredients and stir to combine. Heat for 5 minutes to dissolve sugar, cool and then pour mixture over tuna.

Marinate mixture overnight. Remove tuna and strain marinade. Retain vegetable mixture to use as a garnish and whisk liquid, keeping it cold, to use as the dressing.

In the photo, tuna has been overlapped in a mould to create a shape before being turned out onto the plate.

Serves 4

Recipe prepared by Martin Bosley
Brasserie Flipp
Wellington

Wine: Ata Rangi Martinborough Petrie Chardonnay 1998

Chardonnay on Golden Sands

Nelson and Marlborough

After crossing Cook Strait on the ferry, the traveller disembarks at Picton, gateway to the South Island and to the Marlborough district.

Marlborough's sunny dry climate is ideal for viticulture, and in the past two decades much of the farmland around Blenheim has been transformed into endless rows of vineyards growing grapes for large producers, in particular Montana. But there are also many smaller wineries, one of the better-known ones being Cloudy Bay Vineyards, whose superb wines are under the direction of chief winemaker Kevin Judd. Cloudy Bay's delicious sauvignon blanc is the perfect accompaniment to a plate of mouthwatering mussels, sourced fresh daily from the mussel farms of the Marlborough Sounds. And certainly not all of the region's pastureland has been planted into vineyards. As the cheeses from the Marlborough Cheese Co-operative prove, the dairy industry is alive and well here.

From Blenheim, drive south through the early goldmining area of Canvastown and over the Pelorus River, where the traveller from the north is surrounded for the first time by lush green South Island native bush and thigh-booted anglers can be seen casting their rods over the deep pools and rapids below. After crossing the Rai and Whangamoa saddles you reach Nelson city, which stretches ribbon-like around the coast of Tasman Bay. On both sides of the Takaka Hill are beach-studded Golden Bay and the Abel Tasman National Park. Inland from Nelson through the dramatic Richmond and Spooner ranges there is an angler's paradise of rivers and lakes.

Nelson, too, has an ideal climate for wine production, and its north-facing slopes are dotted with boutique wineries such as Neudorf Vineyards, owned by Tim and Judy Finn, whose small but high-quality wine production is in great demand from restaurants in this country and abroad. Try their delightful 1999 chardonnay at Mapua Wharf's Nature Smoke Café – the perfect partner to the café's hot-smoked salmon. Nelson also sports a flourishing fishing industry, and the orchards are overflowing with juicy apples and luscious berry fruit.

Nestled in this mountain-ringed haven is a large coterie of creative talent, including accomplished silversmiths, painters, glassworkers, potters, weavers, sculptors, woodcarvers and ceramic artists. The region's sunny, cloudless skies provide a clarity of light and colour that has attracted many well-known painters over the years. Colin McCahon painted here in his youth, and the late Sir Tosswill Woollaston spent much of his life in the Nelson district.

Scallops on Watercress

a salad with roasted tomatoes, crème fraîche and garlic croutons

¹/₂ cup cream
¹/₂ cup sour cream

36–42 scallops (depending on size)
2–3 tablespoons sesame oil
salt and lemon pepper

3 tomatoes
pinch sugar, salt and freshly ground black pepper
2–3 tablespoons olive oil
1–2 tablespoons balsamic vinegar

75g butter
3 cloves garlic, peeled and finely chopped
¹/₂ French stick, cut into cubes

sweet chilli sauce and chopped coriander to garnish

Whip cream, add sour cream and mix. Cover with gladwrap and leave in warm place overnight, then chill.

Pan-fry scallops in a little hot sesame oil. Season with a pinch of salt and lemon pepper.

Cut tomatoes in half, sprinkle with a little salt, pepper and sugar and drizzle with olive oil and balsamic vinegar. Bake at 180°C for 8 minutes and then lower heat to 120°C and bake for a further 15 minutes.

Melt butter in a frypan and add garlic.

Fry bread in garlic butter.

Place on a baking tray and crisp in a hot oven for 3 minutes at the same time as the tomatoes.

Make watercress salad with watercress and a few other mixed salad leaves.

Assemble as in photo.

Serves 6

Recipe prepared by Michael Wright
WALNUT CAFÉ
RICHMOND

Wine: Himmelsfeld Sauvignon Blanc
1999

Above: The entrance gate to painter Jane Evans's house in Nelson, made from welded metal by local sculptor Glen van de Leij.

Chapter opening page: Little Kaiteriteri in Golden Bay, Nelson.

Right: *Zanzibar Woman 100% Hair,* created by Andrea Clinton, Nelson, won the Recycle Redress section of the 1997 Montana Wearable Art Awards. The Awards began in 1987 as a small fundraiser. Over the years the show has expanded under the direction of sculptor Susie Moncrieff and the sponsorship of Montana Wines to become a theatrical pageant attracting an audience of more than 5000.

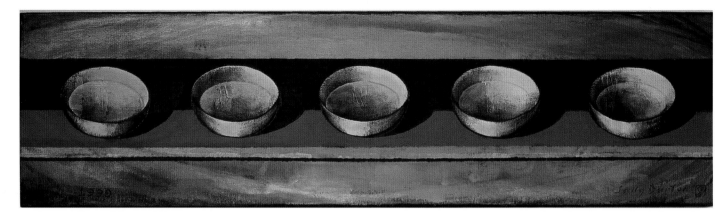

Above: The Length of the Day, acrylic on canvas by Nelson painter Sally Burton.

Below: Sally Burton's *Antipodean Bounty*, also acrylic on canvas.

Swiss Chocolate Mousse

with seasonal fruit and whipped cream

1½ leaves gelatine
500g cream
200g dark Swiss chocolate couverture or dark compound chocolate
3 eggs
100g sugar
2 tablespoons liqueur (optional) Cointreau, Kahlua, etc

Soak gelatine leaves in cold water until soft. Whip cream (and optional liqueur) firmly and keep cool in fridge. Melt dark chocolate in microwave on High for about 30 seconds.

Mix eggs and sugar and whisk thoroughly in a bowl over boiling water until mixture is hot and fluffy (using an electric handheld beater makes this easier).

Remove from heat and add softened, drained gelatine leaves to hot mixture.

When gelatine is completely dissolved, add melted chocolate and mix.

Keep whisking with the bowl in iced water until mixture is starting to get cold.

Finally fold whipped cream into mixture and chill for 2 hours.

Serve with fresh whipped cream and seasonal fruit.

Serves 6

Recipe prepared by Michael Stosser
AMADEUS
NELSON

Wine: Te Hania Ice Wine

Steamed Whole Paddle Crab

served with warm garlic butter and salad

1 crab per person

For each crab:
1 teaspoon fresh garlic, finely chopped
1 tablespoon butter
salt and freshly ground black pepper to taste

First kill your crab. Turn it upside down so it can't walk away, then with a strong knife exert a firm pressure to force knife, point first, through the indented spot just above the tail flap.

This will kill the crab instantly and humanely. If you can't do this, place the crab in fresh water; this will drown it in about 10 minutes.

In the meantime, put a large pot with about 50mm of water on to boil.

Place crab in boiling water and put a lid on pot to steam crab.

A crab needs to steam for about 10 minutes. Be careful not to boil the pot dry, unless you want smoked crab!

Next, place the pot with the crab in it under the cold tap to cool the crab enough so you can handle it.

When cool enough, hold crab by the back paddle legs and with shell facing you, lift shell off, tipping it from the back paddle legs end. It should come off easily. Next, wash gills and guts out.

Either using your hands or a knife, divide crab into quarters and start eating.

To get meat out of legs easily, cut leg just below the joint, then squeeze meat out.

Serve with warm garlic butter and a fresh garden salad.

Can also be served with a sweet chilli sauce or aioli.

Recipe prepared by Cole Ryan
THE BOATSHED
NELSON

Wine: Neudorf Sauvignon Blanc 1999

Caper-crusted Salmon

with lime and parmesan flavours and
a crisp green salad

1¹/₂ cups capers, drained and squeezed dry
³/₄ cup fresh parmesan, grated
rind of 4 small limes
4 x 250g–300g portions of hot smoked
salmon skin on, boned

To make crust, process drained capers in a
food processor until finely chopped but not
pulverised. Add parmesan and lime zest
and mix through.

Lay salmon portions on oven tray. Pile
crust on top of salmon and spread over
evenly.

Heat grill and grill salmon until caper
crust crisps and salmon is warmed through
(about 4–5 minutes). Be careful not to
allow salmon to dry out.

Serve with fresh salad greens drizzled
with balsamic vinegar and olive oil
dressing.

Garnish with fresh lime segments.

Serves 4

Recipe prepared by Tersha Coppell
MAPUA NATURE SMOKE CAFÉ
NELSON

Wine: Neudorf Chardonnay 1999

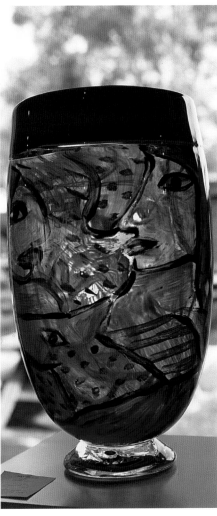

Left: Mapua Nature Smoke Café sits on the wharf at Mapua village, overlooking a shallow backwater where the tide rushes in and out at great speed. Next to the café is the smokehouse and shop whose customers come from all over the region to buy the famous smoked fish pâté.

Below: An example of work by Nelson glassblowers and engravers Ola and Marie Höglund, of Höglund Glassblowing Studio in Nelson. The Höglunds are from Sweden and trained at the famous Orrefors glass school. They settled in Nelson in 1984.

Seifried Estate's vineyard and restaurant near Rabbit Island, Nelson. Hermann Seifried and his wife Agnes established their first vineyard in the Moutere Valley, between Nelson and Motueka, in 1973. The estate now has the region's largest winery. Its vineyards span 120 acres in three separate locations and its wine is sold throughout New Zealand.

Cellarhands Choice
hot honey and lemon chicken, mango, cashews and tomato salsa between char-grilled flatbreads

600g sliced chicken breast (skin off)
2 tablespoons sesame oil
salt and freshly ground black pepper
juice from 1 lemon
½ cup liquid honey
4 flatbreads or pita breads
1 fancy lettuce
100g roasted cashew nuts
1 tin mango slices, drained
4 dessertspoons spicy tomato chutney
100g basil pesto
½ cup olive oil

Stir-fry chicken in hot sesame oil, and add salt and pepper. Cook until golden brown, add lemon juice and honey.

Cook on low heat for 3–4 minutes.

Slice flatbreads in half and char-grill.

Put lettuce on bread half, sprinkle cashews over, cover with mango slices and top with chicken and tomato chutney.

Mix basil pesto with olive oil and pour this dressing over it.

Then close with the other half of the bread.

Garnish with chive flowers and chives.

Serves 4

Recipe prepared by Rene Habets
SEIFRIEDS
RICHMOND

Wine: Seifried Nelson
Gewürztraminer 1999

Savoy Lamb Rack

served with golden kumara, pea and mint
salsa and braised savoy cabbage

4 racks of New Zealand lamb
4 kumara, blanched, sliced and roasted

Braised Cabbage
4 medium shallots, finely sliced
3 rashers bacon, finely sliced
1 tablespoon cumin seeds
1 small savoy cabbage, finely sliced
2 tablespoons butter

Pea and Mint Salsa
1 cup peas
4 spring onions, finely sliced
1/2 cup mint, finely sliced
1/2 cup good quality olive oil

Lamb Jus
1 cup finely chopped mirepoix of vegetables
(carrot, celery, onion)
3 cloves garlic
2 cups good quality lamb stock

Trim lamb racks, removing silverskin and
fat (but leave a little fat to keep meat moist
while cooking). Season meat and seal in a
hot pan. Transfer to a hot oven and cook to
required degree (best served medium-rare).
Allow to rest before serving.

For cabbage, cook shallots, bacon and
cumin seeds without browning. Blanch
cabbage in boiling, salted water and refresh
in iced water. Add shallots, bacon and
cumin seeds to cabbage and mix through.
Reheat with butter and season to taste.

For pea salsa, blanch peas in boiling,
salted water and refresh in iced water. Blitz
peas in food processor to break up slightly.
Put in bowl with spring onions and mint.
Add olive oil and season to taste.

For lamb jus, cook vegetables and garlic
without browning. Add stock. Reduce to
required consistency. Pass through a fine
sieve and season to taste.

Present as in photo.

Serves 4

Recipe prepared by Chris Fortune
HOTEL D'URVILLE, BLENHEIM

Wine: Seresin Pinot Noir 1998

Strutting Rooster with Audience
Entranced, gouache and watercolour,
by Jane Evans. This painting hangs in
the dining room of
the artist's Nelson home.

Screenprinted pillowcases featuring
nikau palm and koru (coiled fern
shoot) design by Nelson artist
Jenny Barraud.

Red Berryfruit Jelly
with fresh strawberries and a fruit coulis

375g caster sugar
500ml Marlborough pinot noir
3 star anise
*4 teaspoons gelatine dissolved in 125ml of hot
red wine syrup (see below) or 6 leaves of
gelatine soaked in cold water to soften*
1 punnet raspberries
1 punnet strawberries
1 punnet blackberries
1 punnet blueberries

To make red jelly, put sugar and red wine
into a saucepan with star anise and melt
sugar over a gentle heat. Take off the heat.
Either dissolve powdered gelatine in 125ml
of the hot syrup and then add to remainder
of syrup or, if using leaf gelatine, add
softened gelatine to the full amount of
syrup and leave to cool but not set.

Arrange a layer of raspberries on the
bottom of six dariole moulds. Pour over a
little jelly and put in refrigerator to set.
Then add a layer of thinly sliced strawberries, more jelly, a layer of blackberries
and blueberries mixed, more jelly and
repeat with strawberries and jelly as a final
layer. Allow to set each time between
layers.

Refrigerate for 2 hours.

To serve, turn jelly out onto a plate (dip
moulds briefly in hot water).

Accompany with berry fruit coulis and
blackberries and raspberries around the
jellies.

Serves 6

Recipe prepared by Jeremy Jones
An Epicurean Affair
Blenheim

Hunter's Chef Salad

with saffron aioli

Saffron Aioli
2 egg yolks
a few threads of saffron
1 teaspoon mustard
1 teaspoon paprika
1½ cups oil
salt and freshly ground black pepper
lemon juice to taste

1 large-leafed lettuce
3 hard-boiled eggs, sliced
3 tomatoes, cut in wedges
2 sticks celery, diced
1 cucumber, sliced
1 cup crispy bacon lardons (diced bacon)
salt and pepper crostini
shaved parmesan cheese

Process egg yolks, saffron threads, mustard and paprika in a food processor.

Then, with the processor on high, carefully add oil drop by drop.

When mixture begins to thicken you can add the oil in a thin stream until it is all used. Add salt and pepper and lemon juice to taste.

Pile lettuce leaves onto the centre of a large plate. Place other ingredients around and on top of lettuce. Top with parmesan cheese and drizzle with Saffron Aioli.

Serves 6

Recipe prepared by Belinda Vavasour
HUNTER'S VINEYARD
BLENHEIM

Wine: Hunter's Sauvignon Blanc 1999

Opposite: Hunter's Wines, Marlborough. Hunter's was established in 1981 by Ernie and Jane Hunter. Since Ernie's tragic death in a motor accident in 1987 Jane has continued his vision. The winery has gone from strength to strength and Jane has become one of the best-known women in the industry. Hunter's present winemaker is Gary Duke.

Below: Blue-glazed ceramic bowl by Nelson artist Christine Boswijk. Behind is the Waimea estuary.

Terranean Bouillabaise

an adaption of a classic seafood soup using
local seafood

50ml extra virgin olive oil
50g each onion, leek, celery, fennel bulb,
finely diced
4 cloves garlic, crushed
12 very ripe, organic tomatoes, chopped
250ml good, bought, fish stock
150ml good quality dry white wine
1 medium to large potato, peeled and sliced

16 live, debearded and scrubbed mussels
1 crayfish tail, cut into 4 equal pieces, or
substitute with shrimps and prawns

600g fresh fish fillets (e.g. gurnard,
monkfish, brill, butterfish), at least
3 different sorts, seasoned with sea salt,
white pepper and lemon juice,
cut in 50g pieces

a pinch of saffron threads
16 scallops
12 shucked oysters
salt and freshly ground black pepper to taste
1 dash pernod (optional)
2 tablespoons fresh herbs (e.g. parsley, dill,
thyme, tarragon), finely chopped

Put first three ingredients in a large, heavy
pot and sauté for about 5 minutes.

Add tomatoes, fish stock, 100ml of the
white wine and potato. Bring to the boil
and cook for about 15 minutes or until
potato is soft and stock has reduced and
thickened up a bit. Put this into a blender
or food processor, taking care not to burn
yourself. Blend to a fine purée and push
through a fine sieve.

Meanwhile steam mussels with the rest
of the white wine in large, heavy pot until
they open (about 5 minutes). Add crayfish
pieces, strained tomato stock and fish
pieces. Simmer gently for a further 5–10
minutes or until fish and crayfish are just
cooked. With a slotted spoon, lift all
seafood out of stock and put equal amounts
into four soup bowls. Keep warm.

Meanwhile, bring tomato stock back to a
boil and add saffron, scallops and, if using,
shrimps and prawns. After 1 minute add
oysters, season to taste and add a dash of

pernod (optional). Spoon this over fish, mussels and crayfish and sprinkle with fresh herbs. Serve immediately with slices of French baguette.

Serves 4

Recipe prepared by Lothar Greiner
MARLBOROUGH TERRANEAN
RESTAURANT
PICTON

Wine: Fromm La Strada Rosé 1999

Above: Sterling-silver pendants by Nelson silversmith Jens Hansen. Jens was one of the pioneers of goldsmithing and silversmithing as an art form in this country. His workshop, established in 1966, has been a training ground for some of New Zealand's leading jewellery makers. Jens died in 1999 but his son Thorkild has continued to produce his own fine jewellery from the studio in Cathedral Square.

Below: Tornio, created by Letty MacPhedran and Barry Keenan from Nelson, one of the winners in the Montana Wearable Art Awards.

Mussel Boys Steamers™ and Flats™

olive oil
16 whole shell mussels
1 tablespoon chopped fresh herbs
(e.g. oregano, thyme, parsley)
¼ cup dry white wine
1 teaspoon chopped fresh garlic
½ cup diced or thinly sliced onions

Heat a pot with a tight-fitting lid on full heat, add a few drops of olive oil and drop in mussels. Sizzle for a few seconds, tossing around. Add all other ingredients as quickly as possible and toss.

Place lid on pot and give a good shake. Leave for 5–6 minutes without lifting lid. Lift lid and check if all mussels have opened. Cook for a minute longer if not ready.

Serve in Steamers™ pot. Place all mussels open side up and pour over broth to half-fill bowl.

Discard any mussels that are tight shut.

Garnish with chopped parsley and lemon wedges. Serve with bread.

(If you are having many discards, allow 2 or 3 extra mussels at start.)

Serves 1

Recipe prepared by Shelly Witchalls
MUSSEL BOYS RESTAURANT
HAVELOCK

Wine: Framingham Chardonnay 1998

Flats with Satay Sauce

Steam open 12–16 mussels per person, depending on size and appetite, in a little water and wine and shuck top shell. Place on the half shell the following sauce as a grill topping.

1 red onion
1 teaspoon fresh minced ginger
1 teaspoon lemongrass, minced, or 1 teaspoon Thai green curry paste
2 cloves garlic
2 teaspoons minced chilli
1 teaspoon Thai fish sauce
1 cup smooth peanut butter
1 cup water
1 tablespoon soy sauce
1 tablespoon chopped fresh coriander
1 cup coconut milk

Blend first five ingredients and sauté over moderate heat until soft. Add remaining ingredients, simmering until a ketchup consistency. Spread 1–2 teaspoons on each mussel half shell and grill for 1–2 minutes. This sauce will store in the refrigerator.

Serves 6

Recipe prepared by Shelly Witchalls
MUSSEL BOYS RESTAURANT
HAVELOCK

The Wild West

West Coast

The West Coast region sits upon the tectonic plate that runs the length of the South Island, a geological phenomenon that produces gold, glaciers and, of course, earthquakes. Here Mother Nature can be a fearsome goddess.

After passing through the narrow Buller Gorge, the traveller arrives at a coastline fringed with strips of pastureland that alternate with clumps of nikau palms and tree ferns. Higher up, jagged rock outcrops like towering castles thrust upwards from dense forests of rata and mountain beech. At Punakaiki in the north, the sea has moulded the limestone into odd pancake-shaped rocks and raging blowholes, and all round the coastline waves break onto driftwood-scattered beaches sending out an aureole of fine spray that merges with the mist from the damp bush and streams above. After heavy rain the rivers become raging torrents pouring from the steep hillsides into the sea and can quickly back up and flood the valleys when they meet an unusually high incoming tide.

But when the weather is warm and sunny and the whitebait are running, river mouths are lined with eager whitebaiters scooping up some of the biggest, juiciest specimens seen anywhere. Meanwhile, more energetic hunters clamber through the beech forests in search of a deer or wild pig to grace the dinner table. This is certainly not wine-producing country, and local diners often prefer a glass of Greymouth's Monteith's lager with their meal to a chardonnay.

The Coast has possibly the smallest population of any region in New Zealand. But tiny settlements like Charleston, Barrytown and Ross were once booming gold towns, their muddy main streets lined with hotels hosting travelling performers and even a three-piece German band. The loud drunkenness of the patrons often indicated another rich strike. Later, when gold fever died out, many of the West Coast towns became distribution centres for the coal mines in the region, but today these, too, have largely been abandoned to history.

In the centre of the region tranquil Lake Brunner, like other Westland lakes, abounds with fat brown trout, To the south the snow-capped Mt Tasman and Mt Cook preside over the ice-blue Fox and Franz Josef glaciers, which plunge from heights of 2600 metres to nearly sea level. Further south the road turns inland through the Gates of Haast, where rounding a bend the traveller is confronted by an awesome body of water, a giant waterfall that tumbles down beside the road so close that you can feel the spray on your skin.

The region may be wild, but it has a flourishing creative culture. Painters, glassblowers and in particular jade carvers draw inspiration from the Coast. Hokitika's greenstone, or nephrite jade, much sought-after by Maori tribes for their adzes, chisels and ornaments, today is equally valued by artists, who carve it into ornaments and jewellery that is sold all over the country.

Venison with Blueberry Sauce

with a mash and stir-fry

*4 x 180g tender venison (back steak or
Denver leg)*
1/2 cup red wine
*1/2 cup game stock (available from good delis
or Gourmet Direct)*
1 cup blueberries
1 tablespoon cold butter

mashed potatoes
vegetable stir-fry

Cut venison into 1–1.5 cm-thick pieces. Cook in a little oil in a hot pan for 2–3 minutes. Remove venison and rest in a warm place.

Add red wine and game stock to cooking pan. Reduce this until it thickens slightly. Pour through a tea strainer into a fresh pan. Add blueberries and simmer. Taste and season. Stir in a knob of cold butter.

Slice venison and serve over a mash and vegetable stir-fry. Pour sauce over. Garnish.

Serves 4

Recipe prepared by
Lynn Browne and Chris Alexander
CAFÉ NEVE
FOX GLACIER

Chapter opening page: Lake Brunner, a gem set amidst high, forest-clad hills, is not accessible by road. But this does not deter anglers, who cross the Arnold River suspension bridge and walk in to the lake's many fishing spots, determined to lure one of its famed large brown trout.

Sautéed Whitebait
with a marinated cherry tomato
and capsicum salad

2 medium kumara
oil for deep-frying
1 tablespoon wholeseed mustard
½ cup red wine vinegar
1 tablespoon honey
⅓ cup olive oil
10 cherry tomatoes, sliced in half
250g whitebait
salt and freshly ground black pepper
2 cups fancy lettuce or mesclun salad mix
2 medium red, yellow or purple capsicums, sliced
Italian parsley

Wash kumara but leave skin on, slice thinly and deep-fry until golden brown.

Drain and place on paper towel.

For vinaigrette, in a bowl place wholeseed mustard, red wine vinegar and honey and mix. Add oil and whisk. Season with salt and pepper.

Slice cherry tomatoes and place in a small pot. Pour over vinaigrette to cover and warm.

Place a pan on high heat and add a touch of oil. When oil starts to smoke, season whitebait with salt and pepper and place in the pan, tossing until cooked (about 40 seconds). Do not overcook or whitebait will become dry.

Arrange lettuce, broken into small pieces, on a plate, alternating with cherry tomatoes and capsicum.

Dress salad with vinaigrette.

In centre of plate place two-thirds of kumara chips, then top with whitebait in a pile.

Garnish top with more kumara chips and the salad with Italian parsley.

Serves 4

Recipe prepared by Craig Fryett
TASMAN VIEW RESTAURANT
HOKITIKA

Above: Woman with pot, a watercolour by West Coast painter
Sue Syme.

Below: Carved pounamu (nephrite jade) ornament by Kai Tahu
carver Turi Gibbs, who lives in Hokitika.

Right: Vase made from
kauri by West Coast
carver Fayne Robinson of
Ngai Tahu and Ngati
Mamoe tribes. The carved
figures (manaia) around the
top of the vase are in the niha
taniwha ('teeth of the taniwha')
design and act as a form of
protection. Round the lower part of
the vase is a contemporary form of
kowhaiwhai, a carving design found
on the rafters of meeting houses.

Whitebait Beignets

with lemon and Thai sweet chilli sauce

225ml water
90g butter
125g flour
3 eggs, lightly beaten
500g whitebait, washed and well drained
1 teaspoon salt
generous grind of black pepper
2 additional egg whites
oil to deep-fry

Put water and butter into a saucepan. Melt butter, then bring to boil.

Throw in sifted flour and stir vigorously until smooth. Cook for a further 2 minutes, stirring so batter does not catch. Cool mixture. Beat in eggs one at a time. Add whitebait, salt and pepper, then fold in additional beaten egg whites to lighten mixture.

Deep-fry spoonfuls of batter in oil until golden and crisp. Drain thoroughly.

Serve hot with lemon or Thai sweet chilli sauce.

Garnish with chives, borage flowers and a sprinkle of salt.

Makes 30–40 beignets
Serves 12 as hors-d'oeuvres, or 6–8 as an entrée

Recipe prepared by
Marian van der Goes
LAKE BRUNNER LODGE
LAKE BRUNNER

Beer: Monteith's Golden Lager

This page: Green-glazed container and
'Nervous Heart' plate by West Coast ceramic
artist Sharon Williams. Originally a tattoo
artist, Sharon Williams's designs are
reminiscent of Maori moko (tattoo) patterns.

Opposite: Some of the Blackball
Salami Company's continental-style
products made from beef and venison
and flavoured with pepperoni and
garlic. The company, founded by two
local butchers, began operating
10 years ago and used to take
samples of new recipes over to the
local pub to be tested by its patrons.
It now has
mail-order customers nationwide.
The building across the road is the
Blackball General Store. Blackball
was established in 1866, and the store
has operated continuously since 1904,
stocking an eclectic mix of goods that
have included gumboots and gold
pans, cast-iron pots, gem irons and
billies, as well as the usual
meat and dry goods.

Crays and Cathedrals

Kaikoura and Canterbury

Driving along the rugged, untamed Kaikoura coast towards Canterbury, the traveller is struck by the huge contrast between these two areas. The rocky coastline feels remote, with no sign of humanity for miles except perhaps a lonely caravan selling fresh crayfish or an early-morning fisher heading out in a small boat to cast a line or set craypots. If you are lucky you may see whales blowing, or perhaps a school of dolphins. Or rounding a headland you might spot a family of seals basking on the rocks below. The Seaward Kaikoura Range, at the northern end of the mighty Southern Alps, towers above the village of Kaikoura like a colossus, especially dramatic in its snowy white winter coat.

But after leaving the coast and climbing over the Hundalees to the Canterbury Plains, the whole scene changes. Around Cheviot, Rangiora and Amberley expanses of pastureland are watched over by stately country houses, while seemingly endless straight roads vanish into the distance. Among the tussock-covered foothills of the Alps are some of New Zealand's great sheep stations, the biggest being Molesworth, whose 1800 square kilometres sprawl over the boundary between North Canterbury and Nelson-Marlborough. On its southern perimeter, along the Lewis Pass route to Nelson, is Hanmer Springs, a nineteenth-century spa town on the edge of a magnificent deciduous forest.

Canterbury's English charm is nowhere more evident than in Christchurch. The Avon River flows through its centre, and in its northern reaches local teams practise throughout the summer for the annual secondary schools boat race. Strolling through Hagley Park, in the centre of the city, you may pass a group of schoolboys from Christ's College in blazers and boaters, giving the illusion that these are the playing fields of Eton. Springtime in the park is a Wordsworthian delight as thousands of daffodils bloom beneath a plethora of English oaks, elms and plane trees more than a century old.

Christchurch's stone buildings around the original Canterbury University campus, now an arts centre housing restaurants, galleries and a theatre complex, are predominantly Gothic in style, and towering over the occasionally bizarre activities of the main city square is the most Gothic of all, the impressive but sombre cathedral. But there are also grand Victorian houses lining the Avon, the 100-year-old Roman Catholic basilica in Renaissance style and many excellent examples of work by contemporary architects. And after gazing at the architecture, one can always go indoors and enjoy the treasures of the Robert McDougall Art Gallery and the Canterbury Museum, next to the famous botanical gardens.

Southwest of Christchurch are the alpine skifields, the largest and most popular being Mt Hutt, and to the northwest is Arthur's Pass, a favourite area for climbers and anglers. The Port Hills in the southeast look over Lyttelton Harbour and further on is the quaint 1840 French settlement of Akaroa, today a haven for artists and craftspeople.

Above: The Kaikoura Wine Company, which commenced operation in 1999, is located on a bluff overlooking the dramatic coastline. Three acres of vineyards surround the winery, but most of its grapes are sourced from Marlborough.

Left: Kaikoura Wines Sauvignon Blanc 1999 is a perfect accompaniment to fresh crayfish.

Karaune, made from feathers, by Canterbury artist Melanie Richardson.

Bangor Estate Cervena and Roasted Figs

Canterbury Cervena with port-roasted figs, chilli-cherry jelly and a zesty herb salad

100ml virgin olive oil
9 small fresh red chillies
4 small red onions, finely sliced
800g Cervena (hind leg cuts are ideal)
200g dried figlets
50ml port wine
150ml balsamic vinegar

Chilli-Cherry Jelly
250g black cherries
50ml port wine
¼ chilli, deseeded and chopped
1½ teaspoons gelatine powder

variety of fresh green herbs, pea vine leaves and lettuce leaves
8 small baked potatoes

Heat half olive oil in a heavy frypan. To hot oil add chillies and coat completely in oil. Cook for about 2 minutes or until skins just begin to blister, then put aside.

For jelly, simmer cherries together with port and chilli until soft. Pass through a coarse sieve, then pass juice though a fine sieve. Heat juices and add dissolved gelatine. Pass again through a fine sieve into a small dish and refrigerate to set.

To hot chilli oil pan, add red onions, toss in oil, cook for 3 minutes and add Cervena, turning quickly to seal all sides of meat. Cook for about 8 minutes or until medium-rare. Add figs, remaining oil then port and vinegar and reduce for 3 minutes.

Remove Cervena, cover and keep warm. Strain figs, onions and oil juices through a coarse sieve. Set figs and onions aside, then pass juices and oil through a fine sieve and keep at room temperature for the glaze.

To serve, arrange salad on serving plate, slice Cervena finely and arrange by overlapping in a single serving mould. Layer, then add a little onion and fig in centre and continue to fill the mould.

Lay sliced baked potatoes in centre of salad and brush with hot olive oil. Turn Cervena out onto potatoes. Brush glaze of

reserved chilli oil and balsamic juices over meat and drizzle remainder over salad. Garnish with red onions, figs, roasted chillies and squares of chilli-cherry jelly.

Serves 4

Recipe prepared by Katie Hill
BANGOR ESTATE
DARFIELD

Wine: Felton Road Pinot Noir 1996

Below: In Sight, an etching by Christchurch artist and printmaker Barry Cleavin.

Bottom right: Library and reading room at the Bangor Estate.

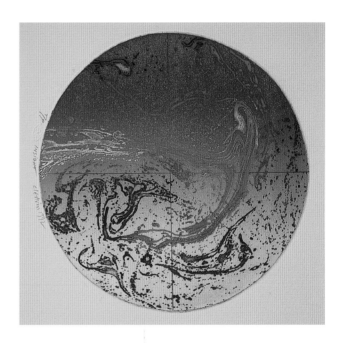

Baked Canterbury Ostrich

local ostrich with herb roasted summer
vegetables and a red capsicum coulis

*4 large red capsicums, deseeded and roughly
chopped*
100ml olive oil
salt and freshly ground black pepper
1 each red, yellow and green capsicum
2 courgettes
1 large eggplant
200g button mushrooms
2 Spanish onions
*2 tablespoons chopped herbs (basil,
coriander, thyme and rosemary)*
2 teaspoons chopped garlic
800g ostrich oyster fillet

Roast the 4 red capsicums in a preheated
oven, 200°C, in a little olive oil for about
15 minutes or until well cooked, then blend
in a food processor for about 2 minutes.
Strain through a fine mesh sieve and
season to taste.

Slice remaining vegetables Chinese-
style, leaving button mushrooms whole or
cut in half if large. Place in roasting tray
with chopped herbs and garlic and
remaining olive oil.

Measure ostrich into 200g portions.
Seal ostrich in a lightly oiled hot pan and
cook in oven at 220°C for 4–8 minutes.
Then put vegetables in for 5 minutes while
ostrich is resting.

Arrange vegetables on a plate, slice
ostrich fillets in two, place on vegetables
and surround plate with warmed capsicum
coulis.

Serves 4

Recipe prepared by Jason Robinson
ANNIES WINE BAR
CHRISTCHURCH

Wine: Mountford Pinot Noir 1998

Pendants and brooch in sterling silver (with gold moon) by Akaroa silversmith
Peter McKay.

Cumin-rubbed Venison
and Moroccan koftas with couscous and a capsicum salad

Spice Rub
50g each cumin and coriander seeds and dried chillies to taste, roasted and ground
1 bay leaf, crushed
1 teaspoon salt and black peppercorns, crushed

1kg pack Denver cut venison, 4 x 120g cuts, remainder for koftas

Koftas
1 medium red onion, chopped
fresh coriander, chopped
4 cloves garlic, crushed
1 egg
½ teaspoon smoked paprika
salt and freshly ground black pepper
sinew-free meat trimmings from venison

1 sprig rosemary
Maldon salt
50ml balsamic vinegar
150ml olive oil
4 mixed capsicums, roasted, peeled, deseeded and petal-cut

200g couscous
200ml hot stock
50g each roasted almonds, dried apricots, currants and butter

To prepare meat, rub combined spices into prime cuts and rest for 1 hour. Mince remainder with onion, coriander, garlic, egg, paprika, seasonings and venison trimmings. Shape around bamboo skewers into 8 meatballs. Set aside on cling film.

To prepare salad, bruise rosemary with salt, blend in vinegar and oil, then sieve and pour over roasted capsicums.

Soak couscous in stock, add fruit, nuts and butter and season with salt and pepper. Keep warm.

To cook meat, sear prime cuts in a little butter until medium-rare. Remove and rest, then add koftas to pan and cook until medium-rare.

Serve as in photo with couscous under venison and salad in front.

The chef serves this dish with a nectarine chutney, a little natural yoghurt and pastry wedges.

Serves 4

Recipe prepared by Bruce Griffiths
COOK'N WITH GAS
CHRISTCHURCH

Wine: Montana Patutahi Estate Gewürztraminer 1998

Pecan-crusted Salmon
salmon over baby greens with a lemon
butter sauce

16 baby potatoes
2 cups pecans, reserve a few for garnish
1 tablespoon garlic, crushed
½ teaspoon salt
¼ teaspoon cayenne
½ cup extra virgin olive oil
8 x 120g portions salmon
4–5 cups vegetables (corn, broccoli,
cauliflower, carrot, etc)
4 heads baby bok choy
1 teaspoon each oil and balsamic vinegar

Preheat oven to 220°C and roast potatoes.

Grind pecans to a coarse meal and add garlic, salt and cayenne. Dip salmon in oil then roll it in nut crumb mixture.

Chill until needed.

Prepare vegetables and bring a large pot of water to boil for blanching them.

When potatoes are almost ready, sear salmon on one side only in a large frypan, then turn onto a shallow roasting dish and finish in the oven for 4–5 minutes or until just cooked.

Meanwhile, blanch vegetables and toss bok choy in oil and vinegar and season.

To serve, place bok choy, then vegetables, on plate, top with salmon and garnish with reserved pecans.

The chef has served this with a lemon/butter sauce.

Serves 8

Recipe prepared by Fred Wieschutter
OGB Restaurant
Christchurch

Plantation Series XVI, oil on canvas by Christchurch painter W.A. (Bill) Sutton. Bill Sutton was particularly well known for his large landscapes depicting the expansive Canterbury Plains, the Port Hills and the grandeur and light of merging sky and land. He died in February 2000 and has left a large body of work spanning five decades.

Benmore Salmon
on a summer salad with a
Thai vinaigrette and crispy noodles

Vinaigrette
1 teaspoon chopped lemon grass
2 tablespoons sweet chilli sauce
3 tablespoons vegetable oil
1 tablespoon spiced vinegar
1 tablespoon sesame oil
1 teaspoon chopped coriander leaves

4 eggs
4 x 200g fresh Benmore salmon fillets
3 tomatoes, quartered
1 cucumber, sliced
2 carrots, peeled and cut into strips
gourmet lettuce, washed, dried and torn into bite-sized pieces
fresh basil and coriander
lemon wedges
200g crispy noodles

Combine all vinaigrette ingredients and whisk.

Whisk eggs and cook omelette-style, then cut into strips. Arrange on plates.

Remove bones from salmon with tweezers or kitchen pliers. Season salmon and seal in hot pan. Place in oven for 8–10 minutes, skin up, until salmon is cooked medium-rare.

Place on salad and generously coat with vinaigrette. Serve with fresh lemon wedges and crispy noodles.

Serves 4

Recipe prepared by Craig Williams
Zanzibar Restaurant
Timaru

Wine: Waipara Springs Sauvignon Blanc 1999

Below: Lyttelton hillside, Canterbury

Lemon Curd Cheesecake
swirls of local lemon curd in an 'Xtraordinary' cheesecake

Base
1 packet wine biscuits
125g melted butter

Filling
2 egg whites
1 cup cream
2 x 250g pottles cream cheese
$^2/_3$ cup sugar
juice of 1 lemon
2 egg yolks
1 tablespoon gelatine dissolved in
2 tablespoons water
1 jar (about 370g) Barkers Lemon Curd

For the base, finely crush biscuits and mix with melted butter. Press into base of a 20cm lined springform tin. Refrigerate for 30 minutes.

For the filling, beat egg whites to soft peaks and set aside.

Beat cream to soft peaks and set aside. In beater combine softened cream cheese and sugar.

Beat until smooth. Add lemon juice, egg yolks and dissolved gelatine. Fold in cream and egg whites. Gently mix lemon curd through. Pour into tin. Leave to set overnight.

Serves 12

Recipe prepared by Robyn Irvine
PLUMS CAFÉ
GERALDINE

Above: A hand-carved bunch of grapes decorates the door of Pegasus Bay Winery in Waipara, North Canterbury.

Below: Pegasus Bay Winery.

Grapes and Goldfields

Central Otago and Queenstown

Central Otago has no officially designated borders, yet the inhabitants are adamant that this it is neither Otago nor Southland. A high plateau crisscrossed by snowcapped mountain ranges and deep gorges, Central experiences clear, icy winters, when brittle branches glisten with hard frost, and hot, dry summers. Cases of frostbite and sunstroke are not uncommon here. But springtime bursts forth in a pageant of blossom and autumn is a rich palette of burnished leaves. Beside the turquoise waters of the always chilly Clutha River grow scented fields of thyme, and in summer there are orchards of luscious apricots, nectarines and peaches.

Bounded in the north by the St Bathans Range and in the west by the Main Divide, Central Otago encompasses lakes Hawea and Wanaka and spreads south as far as the long dog-leg of Lake Wakatipu and the evocatively named Shotover River, a popular stretch of water for jetboating excursions. On Wakatipu's northern shore is the vibrant tourist town of Queenstown, servicing the ski resorts of Coronet Peak and the Remarkables. From there the region extends across the grassy Maniototo Plain as far as the Taieri River.

In 1861 gold was discovered near Lawrence, and gold fever quickly spread up the Clutha River. Large canvas towns sprang up at Clyde and Alexandra and by 1863 there were 10,000 prospectors panning and digging in the area, some of the more hardy pushing up into the lakes district and the Southern Alps.

Cromwell was once a thriving town servicing prospectors from all over the world. Living conditions were often primitive. Exposure, freezing waters and unseasonal snow all claimed their gold-struck victims, as is evidenced by the many Chinese and other foreign names on headstones at the local cemetery.

Historic Arrowtown's main street is lined with old wood and stone cottages and sycamore trees that, in memory of its rich past, blaze with a different kind of gold every autumn. The Clyde dam near Cromwell and an older hydro dam further south at Roxburgh both harness the power of the mighty Clutha, New Zealand's deepest river.

This is the world's most southerly wine region. The gentle valleys have a mellow microclimate similar to that of Tuscany or Burgundy, and their alluvial schist soils and north-facing slopes have recently begun to produce some brilliant wines. Olives are also beginning to take hold here, and there is even a truffière, or truffle farm.

Central is a region of clear light, vibrant colour and dramatic land and skyscapes much favoured by painters, such as Dunedin artists Grahame Sydney and Marilynn Webb, and Tom Field, who now lives in Canterbury. Many have a second home in Central Otago, perhaps an old cottage in Lauder with a picturesque potager garden, a converted shearer's dwelling in Middlemarch, or a mudbrick former railway hotel in the Ida Valley, where they come for weekends and holidays to paint the dramatic, ever-changing landscape.

Above: Beyond the Toscana restaurant lies Lake Wanaka and the peaks of Mt Aspiring National Park.

Opposite: From the front of River Run Lodge at Lake Wanaka, guests can look out over Mt Maude, Mt Gold, the Minarets and Buchanan Peaks.

Chapter opening page: Rippon Vineyard, Lake Wanaka.

Toscana Antipasti
A selection of flavours from Italy

Bruschetta oglio – homemade bread grilled and brushed with garlic-flavoured olive oil. Fegatini and chicken liver pâté* made with capers, anchovies, parsley, wine and garlic glazed carrots, and carrots caramelised with sugar and capers. Selection of cured and dried meats and salamis, fresh fruits and strawberries and rock melon. Mussels in the half shell grilled with tomato and parmesan. Melanzane con pomodoro – eggplants baked in a tomato, herb and garlic sauce. Feta cheese pizza bread – baked in a wood-fired oven, brushed with garlic oil and sprinkled with parmesan.

* Tuscan Chicken Liver Pâté

2 tablespoons canola oil
1 small onion, finely chopped
500g chicken livers
2 tablespoons capers
2 anchovies, chopped (optional)
¼ cup marsala or a sweet red wine
salt and freshly ground black pepper to taste
2–3 tablespoons cream or homemade mayonnaise

Heat oil in a heavy pan and gently fry the onion and chicken livers, being careful not to overcook or the pâté will be bitter.

Add the capers, anchovies and marsala and cook gently for 10–15 minutes.

Squash or chop the livers, then season and add the cream. Mix in and allow to cool. This is a chunky pâté – not the smooth type.

Platter and recipe prepared by
Johanna and Wolfram Guessler
TOSCANA ITALIAN RESTAURANT
WANAKA

Wine: Mount Maude Riesling 1999

Panna Cotta

with grilled nectarines and thyme

Panna Cotta

120g (½ cup) vanilla sugar (prepared earlier)
300g mascarpone cheese
350g sour cream
500ml cream
4 teaspoons gelatine
¼ cup boiling water
juice of 2 small lemons

Grilled Nectarines

4 cups sugar
3 cups water
zest of 1 lemon
fine strips of peel from 2 oranges
6–8 nectarines, halved and stoned
thyme honey and fresh thyme

Pre-prepare vanilla sugar by whizzing in a food processor 1 vanilla bean to 1 cup caster sugar. Sieve and store.

In a steel bowl beat together mascarpone, sour cream and cream with vanilla sugar. Dissolve gelatine in boiling water. Place bowl (with creams) in a double boiler and stir gently until mixture is almost boiling and melted. Stir in lemon juice and gelatine. Heat for 1–2 minutes longer. Ladle into 6–8 (depending on size) lightly oiled ramekins and chill on a tray in refrigerator for 4 hours.

To cook nectarines, slowly bring sugar and water to the boil on a low heat until syrup thickens. Add zest of lemon and orange peel.

Lay nectarines skin side down in an ovenproof dish. Put a tiny swirl of thyme honey and a piece of thyme in each, and pour syrup over .

Grill on a rack in the middle of the oven for approximately 20 minutes or until fruit just begins to brown at edges. Leave for 30 minutes to develop colour in syrup.

To serve, carefully unmould panna cotta and serve with nectarines.

Serves 6–8

Recipe prepared by Meg Taylor
RIVER RUN, WANAKA

Wine: Mt Difficulty Chardonnay 1998

Tia Maria and Nougatine Ice Cream

with seasonal fresh fruit

1 litre cream
150g sugar
200g Tia Maria
4 egg yolks
4 egg whites
50g sugar
150g nougatine, crushed

Berry Coulis
300g frozen berries
½ cup water
100g sugar
2 teaspoons arrowroot

fresh fruit, sliced oranges, strawberries, cape
gooseberries
2 tablespoons passionfruit pulp

To make ice cream, whip cream and set aside. Boil the first measure of sugar and Tia Maria until sugar is dissolved, then whip the egg yolks and pour syrup slowly into yolks, beating until cold and thick. Whip egg whites and second measure of sugar until stiff. Fold into egg yolks, then add to cream and nougatine carefully. Pour into moulds and freeze.

For berry coulis, simmer all ingredients for 5 minutes until sugar is dissolved. Place in a food processor, blend until smooth and sieve.

Note: To make a thicker sauce, dilute arrowroot with cold water, add to saucepan while simmering and stir well.

Arrange as in photo. (The chef has garnished this with spun sugar and a chocolate tuile.)

Serves 4

Recipe prepared by Richard Cross
MILLBROOK
ARROWTOWN

Wine: Montana Virtu Noble
Sémillon 1996

Above: Millbrook Country Club,
near Arrowtown. In the distance
are the snow-covered Remarkables.

Opposite: The Clubhouse
Restaurant at Millbrook overlooks
the eighteenth hole of the golf
course and a small lake.

Above: Twenty kilometres from Queenstown, Chard Farm Vineyard perches on a cliff overlooking the Kawarau Bridge, a popular 'stepping off' point for bungy jumpers. Chard Farm produces a broad range of wine styles, including its top-of-the-range pinot noir, Bragato, and the excellent Judge and Jury Chardonnay, named after the rocky outcrop that towers above the vineyard.

Below: In the grounds of Chard Farm this sculpture in Oamaru stone by Stephanie Jewel evokes bacchanalian pleasures. Along its base are lines from the eleventh-century Persian poet Omar Khayyám: 'Awake my little ones, and fill the cup before life's liquor in its cup be dry.'

Tuna with Tobiko Roe
and wasabi mayonnaise

1 packet Hijiki seaweed
juice of 3 lemons
20 leaves each basil and watercress
150ml canola oil
2 egg yolks
4 tablespoons wasabi powder mixed with
½ cup cold water
150ml canola oil
½ teaspoon palm sugar
Maldon sea salt
cracked pepper
1 fist-sized golden kumara, peeled
200ml canola oil
200g yellowfin tuna
salt and pepper to season
60g Tobiko flying fish roe, assorted colours

Soak Hijiki seaweed in lots of water for 20 minutes, drain. Add juice of 1 lemon.

Blanch basil and watercress leaves for 20 seconds (no more), then cool in iced water. This keeps the herbs a vibrant green. Blend for a minute with first measure of canola oil. Strain through a fine sieve and set aside.

Add juice of remaining 2 lemons to egg yolks and 1 teaspoon of wasabi paste. Slowly whisk in second measure of canola oil. Season with palm sugar, sea salt and two turns of the pepper mill. Set aside.

Slice kumara into matchstick-sized batons. Heat third measure of canola oil in a steep-sided saucepan. When hot, fry kumara until a light tan colour and crisp. Drain on a paper towel.

Season tuna loin with salt and pepper, then char-grill or barbecue for 2 minutes on each side, depending on the thickness of tuna. This dish should be served quite rare.

Place a rounded tablespoon of wasabi mayonnaise in the centre of each plate. Top with quarter of the fried kumara, then thinly slice tuna and fan over kumara nest. Then add a generous pinch of Hijiki seaweed and top with flying fish roe.

Serves 4

Recipe prepared by Peter Gawron
SAFFRON, ARROWTOWN

Wine: Peregrine Sauvignon Blanc 1999

Solera Brûlée
with a toffee swirl

1 litre cream
zest of 1 lemon
1 cup caster sugar
1 vanilla bean, split
13 egg yolks

Toffee
1 cup sugar
¼ cup water

Bring first four ingredients to the boil to dissolve sugar. Whisk egg yolks and combine with cream mixture. Strain into a clean pot. Pour into greased moulds.

Bake in a waterbath for 1½ hours at 150°C.

To make toffee, boil sugar and water until light brown and let cool for a few minutes. Use a spoon to make spirals on a greased, stainless-steel bench. Leave to set.

When serving, place toffee on brûlée.

Serves 8

Recipe prepared by Fleur Langford
SOLERA VINO
QUEENSTOWN

Wine: Felton Road Block 1 Riesling 1999

Solera Vino restaurant and bar, Queenstown. The large decorative pot is by Nelson ceramic artist Christine Boswijk.

Right: Castle Mountain, Clinton Valley, Fiordland, oil on canvas, by Queenstown painter Ivan Clarke.

Opposite page: Rippon Vineyard lies on the shores of Lake Wanaka, with the Buchanan Peaks behind. Rippon is justly proud of its quality range of wine styles, in particular the excellent classic pinot noir. Emma Rippon Méthode Traditionelle was the first bottle-fermented sparkling wine produced in Central Otago. Rippon Vineyard has a Bio-Gro certificate for organic production.

Left: From Vinegar Hill, a Central Otago landscape in oils by Tom Field. The artist now lives in Christchurch but frequently returns to Central Otago for his subject matter.

Chermoulah Tuna
with saffron mash and roasted vegetables

Chermoulah
¹/₄ cup each parsley and coriander
4 mint leaves
¹/₄ teaspoon each cumin and paprika
¹/₄ cup lemon juice
1 clove garlic
pinch salt
1–2 tablespoons oil

Saffron Mash
100ml cream
15 threads saffron
4 portions mashed potato

4 x 180g tuna loin medallions
extra virgin olive oil
2 roasted zucchini, sliced
1 roasted eggplant, sliced
*1 roasted red capsicum, peeled and
cut into four*
¹/₂ cup unsweetened yoghurt

For the chermoulah, blend all ingredients in a food processor, except oil. Add oil last to form a smooth paste. For the saffron mash, heat cream with saffron threads, reduce by half and add to warm mashed potato. Whisk in well until soft and creamy.

Rub tuna medallions in chermoulah paste. Leave to marinate for at least 1 hour.

Seal tuna on high heat and cook in a hot oven for 3 minutes, until medium-rare.

Heat saffron mash and place on plate. Drizzle extra virgin olive oil around mash.

Cut tuna medallions in half. Place one piece, cut side up, on the mash. Put reheated roast vegetables on top of tuna. Drizzle yoghurt on top of vegetables and place other piece of tuna, cut side up, to finish the dish.

Serves 4

Recipe prepared by Andrew Rennie
THE 19TH RESTAURANT
QUEENSTOWN

Wine: Felton Road Vin Gris 1999

Previous page: The 19th restaurant and bar is located on the wharf, Queenstown, near where the pleasure steamer TSS *Earnslaw* takes passengers for excursions on Lake Wakatipu. The *Earnslaw* has been working these waters since 1912, and was not always a pleasure boat. Initially it was used to take supplies to the sheep stations surrounding the lake.

Above: Dunstan Waters, an oil painting by Tom Field.

Left: Bowl with decorative lid in glazed porcelain, by Suzanne Scott Butson from Queenstown.

Right: Wild Thyme and Spring Snow, Maniototo, a hand-coloured monotype engraving by Dunedin artist Marilynn Webb, who spends much of her time in Central Otago.

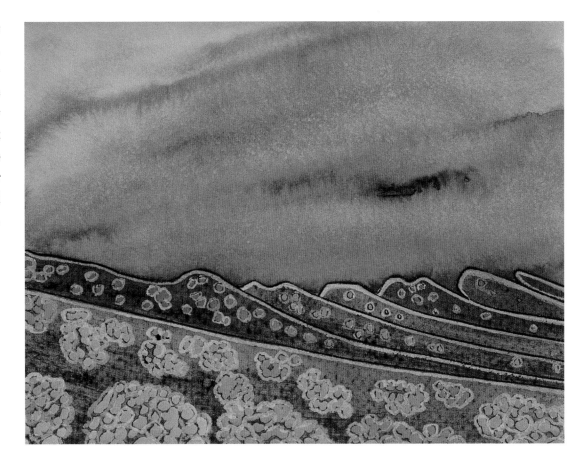

Below: Sign at the entrance to Peregrine Wines vineyard at Wentworth Estate on Kawarau Gorge Road. The company's symbol, depicted in simple form on the sign, is the native peregrine falcon, a spectacular bird that soars above Central Otago's mountains, lakes and rivers.

Toasted and Caramelised Coconut Ice Cream

8 egg yolks
150g caster sugar
500ml cream
300g desiccated coconut
300g caster sugar
200ml cream
500ml cream

Cream egg yolks and first measure of caster sugar. Boil first measure of cream and mix into yolk and sugar mixture. Heat until mixture thickens but do not boil. Cool mixture. Toast coconut.

Put second measure of caster sugar into a pot with a little water and boil until golden brown. Add the 200ml cream and take off the heat. Stir until caramel is smooth.

Pour caramel over coconut and then mix into cooled custard mixture.

Whip final measure of cream and fold into mixture. Make cone shapes from paper, making sure there are no holes for the mixture to run out, and pour mixture into them. Freeze.

Remove paper to serve.

Makes 10–15 cones

Recipe prepared by Bec McLean
OLIVERS RESTAURANT
CLYDE

Wine: Chard Farm Riesling 1999
(recommended wine)

Opposite and below: The old-world garden of Olivers restaurant and lodge in Clyde. Built from stone cut from the Cromwell Gorge, Olivers began operating in 1863 as a general store, supplying dry goods, tea, meat and other essentials to the hordes of gold-seeking prospectors. The original storefront, barn, smokehouse, stables and main house have been preserved and carefully restored.

Scots Baps

with roasted fruit

175ml tepid milk
175ml water
2 teaspoons dried yeast
1 teaspoon sugar
500g strong white flour
1½ teaspoons salt
1 tablespoon milk to glaze

Combine milk and water. Sprinkle yeast and sugar into 100ml of this liquid, leave for 5 minutes and stir to dissolve.

Stir in half the remaining milk/water liquid.

Mix flour and salt together in a large bowl. Make a well in the centre and pour in yeasted milk.

Mix in flour and reserved milk/water as needed to form a sticky dough. Knead for 10 minutes until smooth and elastic. Put dough in a clean bowl, cover and leave to rise until doubled in bulk.

Knock back, then rest for 10 minutes.

Divide dough into eight equal portions.

Shape each piece into a flat oval about 1cm thick and place on a floured baking sheet. Brush with milk and sift over a heavy dusting of flour. Leave to prove, uncovered, until doubled in size, for about 30–40 minutes.

Again sift a heavy dusting of flour over each bap, using your thumb to make an impression about 1cm deep in the centre of each bap.

Bake the baps in a preheated oven for 15–20 minutes. Cover with a tea-towel and leave to cool on a wire rack.

Serve with roasted fruit.

Serves 8

Recipe prepared by Karen Smythe
CONSTABLE COTTAGE AND GAOL
ST BATHANS

Rugged Scots and Bluff Oysters

Otago and Southland

The boundary between Canterbury and Otago officially drawn up in 1861 followed the Ohau and Waitaki rivers from the Southern Alps in the west out to the eastern coastline. But for the past decade or more Otagoites and Cantabrians have been re-enacting their English and Scottish ancestors' border wars, with each regional council making bandit raids on the other's territory. Nevertheless, language speaks louder than officialdom, and affiliations to bonnie Otago depend more on a Scottish burr and the roll of an R than on geography.

The Scottish influence accounts for more than just the accent. It was the Scots that originally settled Dunedin and Invercargill and, being staunch porridge eaters, they made this the only region in the country ever to grow significant crops of oats. The ancient Scottish sport of curling is still practised on shallow frozen lakes, and up until World War II settlers manufactured illicit whisky in the Hokonui Hills behind the Southland town of Gore. Whisky is now made legally at a distillery in Mosgiel.

Gold was first discovered in the region by Gabriel Read in 1861 at what is now called Gabriels Gully, near Lawrence, and in the following year 200,000 ounces were transported from the Central Otago fields into Dunedin's bank vaults by a weekly escort of mounted troopers. This bounty endowed the city's art galleries, university and other cultural icons and provided much of the funding to develop the region's agricultural resources – wool, wheat and meat. New Zealand's first shipment of frozen meat

left Otago Harbour in 1882, bound for Britain on board the *Dunedin*.

Dunedin's architecture is a delightful mix of Edwardian public buildings made from Oamaru stone and bluestone, and quaint Victorian brick terrace-houses trimmed with iron trellis. The Otago Peninsula, overlooked by Larnach's Castle, built for nineteenth-century parliamentarian William Larnach, has attracted to its shores not only colonies of royal albatrosses and yellow-eyed penguins, but also small galleries and a settlement of artists and craftspeople.

South of Dunedin is the dramatic Catlins State Forest Park, which is surrounded by large sheep runs and backed by the Maclennan Range. To the west is the city of Invercargill, where the Southland Museum and Art Gallery houses objects salvaged from early shipwrecks and relics from sealing and whaling days, while outside stands a section of fossilised forest that is 160 million years old.

Just south of Invercargill is Bluff, New Zealand's southernmost town, from which comes the much-coveted giant oysters. During their short season these are flown to tables all around the country.

In the western part of this region are Lake Te Anau and the much-photographed still waters of Lake Manapouri in Fiordland National Park. Out towards the coast the road stops at the remote Milford Sound. This is the only fiord accessible by road. Often painted by New Zealand's nineteenth-century masters, the steep, bushclad Fiordland coast is virtually uninhabited.

Cervena Pithivier with Pot Roast

a quick pot-roast venison and a special pie with baby beets and whole garlic

Venison Pithivier
(prepared 1 day earlier)
1 x 300g (approximately) piece of venison shin
½ cup each of roughly chopped celery, onion and carrot
2 slices pancetta ham
800ml brown stock (venison if possible)
200ml red wine
1 sprig rosemary
10 crushed peppercorns
2 teaspoons wholeseed mustard
6 sheets pre-rolled puff pastry

Braise shin according to your favourite method, using all ingredients apart from mustard. Cook slowly until meat literally falls away from the bone.

Shred meat with a fork and pour over this the braising liquor that has been reduced to approximately 100ml, along with the mustard.

Combine and refrigerate until mix is completely cold before putting it into your puff pastry.

For the pithivier: Cut 6 x 12.5cm discs from the pastry sheets.

Place a good portion of filling in the centre of three of these, egg-wash the edges, put the lid in place and press edges down to seal. Recut edges again with the same pastry cutter to reshape.

Egg-wash and decorate with wagon-wheel knife marks. Return to the refrigerator and let rest for 15 minutes at least. Bake in an oven preheated to 200°C until golden brown.

Chapter opening page: Dunedin's Town Hall and Municipal Chambers. The original part of this classic building was designed by R.A. Lawson and completed in 1880. Beside the Town Hall is St Pauls Anglican Cathedral, built in 1915 from Oamaru stone.

Pot Roast

900g piece of farmed venison (well aged),
seared in a cast-iron casserole

1 medium carrot, roughly chopped

2 medium red onions, peeled and sliced into
thick rings

12 whole heads of baby garlic (make a cut
through side of garlic to centre)

18 walnut-sized baby beetroots (steamed for
20 minutes and skin removed)

1 fresh bay leaf

1 sprig lemon thyme

1 teaspoon sugar

1 tablespoon balsamic vinegar

300ml good fresh brown stock

freshly ground black pepper and salt to taste

In the same large cast-iron casserole, braise
the seared venison on the carrot and onion,
adding garlic, beets and herbs. Cover well
and cook at 200°C for 15–20 minutes,
depending on thickness of meat.

Remove meat, beets and garlic and rest
for at least 15 minutes in a warm place
before carving.

Place casserole back on medium heat,
add sugar and allow carrot and onion to
gently caramelise.

Deglaze by adding balsamic vinegar and
then stock. Simmer until sauce has
reduced by half and become glossy. Correct
seasoning, strain into a clean saucepan and
keep hot.

To serve, arrange as shown in the photo,
allowing half a pithivier per person.

Serves 6

Recipe prepared by Michael Coughlin
BELL PEPPER BLUES
DUNEDIN

Wine: Mt Difficulty Chardonnay 1998

Tuscan Rubbed Lamb Loin

upon fragrant couscous,
oven-roasted cherry tomatoes, olives and
pinenuts, drizzled with red capsicum oil

4 lamb shortloins
1 tablespoon rock salt
1 teaspoon sugar
1 teaspoon crushed garlic
½ teaspoon each rosemary, cracked pepper
and chopped parsley
1 tablespoon oil

300g cherry tomatoes
32 pitted olives
2 tablespoons fresh rosemary tips
4 tablespoons pinenuts
1 tablespoon oil

2 red capsicums
½ medium onion, finely chopped
1 clove garlic
pinch each dried thyme and rosemary
1 bay leaf
2 parsley stalks
6 peppercorns
2 tablespoons tomato paste
100ml oil

For the lamb, preheat oven to 190°C. Combine salt, sugar, herbs and oil and rub mix onto lamb prior to cooking. Sear in a hot pan and finish cooking in the oven for 8–10 minutes. Let meat rest for 5 minutes.

For the tomatoes, combine all the ingredients, season with salt and pepper, place in a baking dish and bake in the oven for 8-10 minutes until cooked.

For the red capsicum oil, combine first eight ingredients and sweat over a medium heat to extract flavour. Add tomato paste. Once cooked and tender, add oil and let stand for 1 hour, then decant oil.

The chef serves this with an onion/basil couscous. Garnish the plate with 80ml balsamic vinegar drizzled around, alfalfa and mizuna.

Serves 4

Recipe prepared by Leon Yee
TOTARA BAR & BRASSERIE
OAMARU

Above: The Totara Bar and Brasserie in Thames Street, Oamaru. The building opposite is the town hall and municipal opera house, designed by J.M. Forrester, built from Oamaru stone and completed in 1907. The opening performance at the opera house was given by the Musgrove Opera Company.

Above: What gat ye for your dinner, Lord Randall my son, crayon on paper, by Kathryn Madill, Dunedin.

Below: Lake Mahinerangi, hand-coloured monotype and engraving, by Dunedin artist Marilynn Webb.

Lamb Terrine
with eggplant, courgettes and fennel

1 eggplant
2 courgettes
3 red capsicums
4 outer leaves of Savoy cabbage
1 bulb fennel
5 lamb fillets
6 sundried tomatoes

Garnish
assortment of herbs
slices of peeled tomato
slices of olive and fennel

Cut eggplant and courgettes into strips, season and char-grill.

Roast capsicums, peel and deseed.

Blanch Savoy cabbage leaves, removing any thick stems.

Cook fennel bulb in seasoned water, remove layers and char-grill. Season lamb fillets and cook in a hot skillet until rare or medium-rare (your own preference).

Line a terrine mould or bread tin with glad wrap, then Savoy cabbage.

Layer terrine with eggplant and courgettes at the bottom, using all the ingredients until it is full.

Put a weight on top of the terrine and press in refrigerator for 24 hours.

Remove from mould and slice.

Arrange garnish liberally around plate.

Serves 8–10

Recipe prepared by Rene Klein

RESTAURANT 95

DUNEDIN

Wine: Hays Lake Pinot Noir 1998

Above: In the Manawatta, acrylic on paper, by Dunedin painter John Robinson.

Right: Opposite Two Chefs restaurant in George Street is Dunedin's Knox Church. One of the city's many architectural treasures, it was designed by R.A. Lawson, an artist of considerable reputation who designed many of both Dunedin and Oamaru's outstanding buildings.

Saffron Seafood Risotto
featuring crayfish, prawns and mussels

900ml fish stock, divided
50ml olive oil
½ onion, finely diced
2 cloves garlic, crushed and chopped
250g arborio rice
100ml sauvignon blanc
2 pinches saffron threads
20 mussels, washed and debearded
1 crayfish body, cut into medallions
12 prawns, peeled and deveined
sea salt and freshly ground black pepper
100g butter
fresh herbs to garnish

Bring 700ml of fish stock to the boil. Heat a wide-based pan and add olive oil. Sauté onion and garlic, add rice and stir until coated with oil.

Pour in wine and saffron and when absorbed start to ladle in simmering fish stock, 150ml at a time. Allow rice to absorb liquid before adding more; stir and shake pan frequently to prevent sticking. Meanwhile, steam open mussels with the extra 200ml of stock in a covered pan. Arrange in wide soup bowls.

Add crayfish and prawns with the last ladle of stock.

The rice should be slightly firm and creamy.

Season with sea salt and freshly ground pepper.

Remove from heat and stir in chopped butter with a wooden spoon. Garnish with fresh herbs.

Serves 4

Recipe prepared by
Helen Mason and Grant Cockroft

2 CHEFS

DUNEDIN

Wine: Felton Road Riesling 1998

Chicken and Avocado Salad

with a pumpkin and passionfruit compote

4 medium-sized chicken breasts, skin removed
2 teaspoons chilli powder
4 teaspoons paprika
¼ small pumpkin (seeds retained and roasted separately)
4–5 passionfruit or passionfruit pulp
2 ripe avocados
1 bag assorted salad leaves
1 thinly sliced red capsicum
1½ cups diced melon
zest and juice of 1 lemon
5 teaspoons olive oil
1 kumara, cut into wafer-sized slices and deep-fried
pumpkin seeds, optional
fresh coriander, optional

Sprinkle chicken breasts with chilli powder and paprika. Bake at 180°C for 15–20 minutes. Allow to cool. Cook pumpkin until soft. Drain well and blend with passionfruit. Place in refrigerator.

Cut avocados in half lengthwise, removing skin and stone. Thinly slice across the breadth and arrange on plates in a semi-circle.

Toss sliced chicken, salad leaves, capsicum, melon, lemon juice and zest, and olive oil in a bowl, then arrange in middle of avocado. Spoon passionfruit compote around salad and garnish with kumara chips, pumpkin seeds and fresh coriander if available.

Serves 4

Recipe prepared by Trish Boyes
GAZEBO RESTAURANT & BAR
GORE

Sweet Island Paradise, acrylic on canvas, by Southland artist Josh McMillan.

Ostrich Medallions

on a potato cake with wilted spinach in a
light mushroom broth

1 litre good chicken stock
200g mushrooms (mixture of white, brown,
shiitake)
4 medium potatoes (Nadine or similar)
10g wasabi powder
3 shallots, finely chopped
70g butter, divided
70ml olive oil, divided
4 x 150g ostrich medallions, cut from the
oyster, supreme or long fillet
Maldon sea salt and freshly ground black
pepper
2 packets spinach, washed and stalks
removed
100g pancetta, julienned
1 each green and yellow courgette, ribbon cut

Place chicken stock in a saucepan and
bring to a simmer. Clean, trim and chop
mushrooms. Add trimmings to stock. Peel
and grate potatoes and rinse under cold,
running water. Squeeze out water.

Add wasabi powder, chopped shallots,
salt and pepper and mould into four
portions.

Heat 50g of the butter and 50ml of the
olive oil in a heavy-based frypan and add
potato. Cook for 4 minutes on a medium
heat and turn. Cook for a further
4 minutes or until cooked.

When potato cakes are almost cooked,
add chopped mushrooms to pan and
quickly toss to cook.

Brush ostrich medallions with olive oil
and season with Maldon sea salt and
freshly ground pepper. Heat a second
heavy-based pan and seal meat until well
coloured. Cook until medium-rare, then
remove from pan and cover with a towel to
let medallions rest for 5 minutes.

Add washed spinach to pan and toss
until wilted. Season with salt and pepper.

Assemble as in photo and garnish with a
stir-fry of vegetables and pancetta.

Recipe prepared by Graham Hawkes
DONOVAN RESTAURANT
INVERCARGILL

Wine: Black Ridge Chardonnay 1999

Hogget Chilli Chops
with mint chutney and a vegetable bake

Mint Chutney (made 10 days in advance)
500g each ripe tomatoes and apples
6 onions
1½ cups seeded raisins
1 cup chopped mint leaves
3 cups vinegar
2 cups sugar
2 teaspoons each mustard and salt

Mince tomatoes, apples, onions, raisins and add finely chopped mint. Scald vinegar, add sugar and seasoning. When cool add minced ingredients. Mix well. Put in jars and keep for at least 10 days before use.

Hogget Chilli Chops
10 chops
1 tablespoon chilli sauce
½ tablespoon crushed garlic
6 tablespoons soy sauce
2 tablespoons each brown sugar and tomato sauce

Vegetable Bake
4–5 cooked, sliced potatoes
1 onion sautéed in 1 tablespoon butter
1 cup each cooked, diced carrot and broccoli
1 tomato, sliced
½ cup chopped spinach
1 cup thinly sliced courgettes
1 teaspoon each basil and oregano
4–5 eggs
½ cup milk
1 tablespoon flour
salt and freshly ground black pepper
grated cheese

Pour chilli, garlic, soy sauce, sugar and tomato sauce over chops and bake for 2 hours at 125–150°C. To cook vegetables, place vegetables and herbs in an ovenproof dish. Beat eggs, milk, flour, salt and pepper together and pour over vegetable mixture. Cover with grated cheese. Bake at 180°C for about 30 minutes. Serve with chops, mint chutney and a carrot salad. Serves 4–6, depending on chop size.

Recipe prepared by June Stratford

CATLINS FARMSTAY
PROGRESS VALLEY, TOKANUI

Artists, Agents and Outlets

(in alphabetical order, by artist, followed by page number)

Restaurant Directory

NORTHLAND & AUCKLAND

Kingfish Lodge, Kingfish Cove, Kaeo, Whangaroa Harbour. Ph (09) 405-0164.

Waikokopu Café, Treaty Grounds, Waitangi. Ph (09) 402-6275.

The Marsden Estate, Wiroa Rd, Kerikeri. Ph (09) 407-9398.

Killer Prawn, 26/28 Bank St, Whangarei. Ph (09) 430-3333.

Morris & James Pottery & Tileworks, 48 Tongue Farm Rd, Matakana. Ph (09) 422-7116.

The Hunting Lodge, Matua Winery, Waikoukou Valley Rd, North West Auckland. Ph (09) 411-8259.

Euro Restaurant, Shed 22, Princes Wharf, Quay St, Auckland. Ph (09) 309-9866.

Vinnies Restaurant, 166 Jervois Rd, Herne Bay, Auckland. Ph (09) 376-5597.

Partingtons, Sheraton Hotel, 83 Symonds St, Auckland. Ph (09) 379-5532.

Café Pacifique at the Carlton Hotel, cnr. Mayoral Dr & Vincent St, Auckland. Ph (09) 366-5626.

Iguacu Restaurant & Bar, 269 Parnell Rd, Parnell, Auckland. Ph (09) 358-4804.

Stonyridge Vineyard, 80 Onetangi Rd, Waiheke Island. Ph (09) 372-8822.

Mudbrick Vineyard & Restaurant, Church Bay Rd, Oneroa, Waiheke Island. Ph (09) 372-9050.

Saints Waterfront Brasserie, 425 Tamaki Dr, St Heliers, Auckland. Ph (09) 575-9969.

Five City Rd Restaurant, 5 City Rd, Auckland Central. Ph (09) 309-9273.

COROMANDEL, BAY OF PLENTY & EAST CAPE

Puka Park Lodge, Mount Ave, Pauanui Beach, Coromandel. Ph (07) 864-8088.

Shells Restaurant & Bar, 227 Main Rd, Tairua, Coromandel. Ph (07) 864-8811.

Mills Reef Winery, Moffat Rd, Bethlehem, Tauranga. Ph (07) 576-8844.

Somerset Cottage, 30 Bethlehem Rd, Bethlehem, Tauranga. Ph (07) 576-6889.

Solitaire Lodge, Ronald Rd, Lake Tarawera, Rotorua. Ph (07) 362-8208.

Memories Restaurant, Princes Gate Hotel, 1057 Arawa St, Rotorua. Ph (07) 348-1179.

Bushmere Arms, cnr State Highway 2 & Bushmere Rd, Gisborne. Ph (06) 862-5820.

Acton Estate, 577 Back Ormond Rd, Gisborne. Ph (06) 867-9999.

Café Villaggio, 57 Ballance St, Gisborne. Ph (06) 868-1611.

WAIKATO, CENTRAL PLATEAU & TARANAKI

The Narrows Landing, 431 Airport Rd, Tamahere, Hamilton. Ph (07) 858-4001.

Tables On The River, 12 Alma St, Hamilton. Ph (07) 839-6555.

The Gallery, 64c Victoria St, Cambridge. Ph (07) 823-0999.

Huka Lodge, Huka Falls Rd, Taupo. Ph (07) 378-5791.

The Brantry Restaurant, 45 Rifle Range Rd, Taupo. Ph (07) 378-0484

The Grand Chateau, Whakapapa Village, Mt Ruapehu. Ph (07) 892-3809.

Backstage Café, 234 Broadway, Stratford, Taranaki. Ph (06) 765-7003.

Mountain House Motor Lodge, Pembroke Rd, East Egmont, Stratford. Ph (06) 765-6100.

HAWKE'S BAY & MANAWATU

Vavasseur Restaurant, 201 Broadway Ave, Palmerston North. Ph (06) 359-3167.

Anatoles, The County Hotel, 12 Browning St, Napier. Ph (06) 835-7800.

Mangapapa Lodge, 466 Napier Rd, Havelock North. Ph (06) 878-3234.

Vidal Estate Winery, 913 Saint Aubyn Street East, Hastings. Ph (06) 876-8105.

The McDonald Winery, 150 Church Rd, Taradale. Ph (06) 844-2053.

Take 5 Wine & Jazz Bar, 189 Marine Parade, Napier. Ph (06) 835-4050.

RD1 Restaurant, Sileni Estates Winery, 2016 Maraekakaho Rd, Hastings. Ph (06) 879-8768.

Crab Farm Winery, 511 Main Rd, Bay View, Napier. Ph (06) 836-6678.

WAIRARAPA & WELLINGTON

Aylstone Private Lodgings, Wine Library & Larder, Huangarua Rd, Martinborough. Ph (06) 306-9505.

Wharekauhau Country Estate, Western Lake Rd, Palliser Bay, Featherston. Ph (06) 307-7581.

Toads Landing, Homebush, Masterton. Ph (06) 377-3793.

Bubbles Bistro, 50 Amohia St, Paraparaumu. Ph (04) 298-3181.

Boulcott St Bistro, Plimmer House, 99 Boulcott St, Wellington. Ph (04) 499-4199.

Logan Brown Restaurant, 192 Cuba St, Wellington. Ph (04) 801-5114.

Dockside Restaurant & Bar, Shed 3, Queens Wharf, Wellington. Ph (04) 499-9900.

The Whitehouse Restaurant, 232 Oriental Parade, Oriental Bay, Wellington. Ph (04) 385-8555.

Brasserie Flipp, 103 Ghuznee St, Wellington. Ph (04) 385-9493.

NELSON & MARLBOROUGH

Walnut Café, 251 Queen St, Richmond, Nelson. Ph (03) 544- 6187.

Amadeus Café & Brasserie, 284 Trafalgar St, Nelson. Ph (03) 545-7191.

The Boat Shed Café, 350 Wakefield Quay, Nelson. Ph (03) 546-9783.

Mapua Nature Smoke, Shed 3, Mapua Wharf, Nelson. Ph (03) 540-2280.

Seifrieds Vineyard Restaurant, Redwood Rd, Appleby, Richmond. Ph (03) 544-1555.

Hotel D'Urville, 52 Queen St, Blenheim. Ph (03) 577-9945.

An Epicurean Affair, Stone Aerie Estate, Dog Point Rd, Blenheim. Ph (03) 572-9639.

Hunters Wines NZ Ltd, Rapaura Rd, Blenheim. Ph (03) 572-8489.

Marlborough Terranean Restaurant, 31 High St, Picton. Ph (03) 573-7122.

The Mussel Boys Restaurant, 73 Main Rd, Havelock. Ph (03) 574-2824.

WEST COAST

Café Neve, Main Rd, Fox Glacier. Ph (03) 751-0110.

Tasman View Restaurant, Southland Hotel, 111 Revell St, Hokitika. Ph (03) 755-8344.

Lake Brunner Lodge, Mitchells, Lake Brunner, Kumara, Westland. Ph (03) 738-0163.

KAIKOURA & CANTERBURY

Bangor Country Estate, Bangor Rd, Darfield, Canterbury. Ph (03) 318-7588.

Annies Wine Bar & Restaurant, Fine Arts Centre, Christchurch. Ph (03) 365-0566.

OGB Restaurant, The Heritage Hotel, 28 Cathedral Square, Christchurch. Ph (03) 363-0895.

Cook'n with Gas, 23 Worcester Boulevard, Christchurch. Ph (03) 377-9166.

Plums Café, 44 Talbot St, Geraldine. Ph (03) 693-9770.

Zanzibar Restaurant & Bar, 56 The Bay Hill, Timaru. Ph (03) 688-4367.

CENTRAL OTAGO & QUEENSTOWN

River Run, Halliday Rd, Wanaka. Ph (03) 443-9049.

The Clubhouse Restaurant, Millbrook Country Club, Malaghan Rd, Arrowtown. Ph (03) 441-7004.

Saffron, 18 Buckingham St, Arrowtown. Ph (03) 442-0131.

Olivers of Clyde, 34 Sunderland St, Clyde, Central Otago. Ph (03) 449-2860.

Solera Vino Restaurant, 25 Beach St, Queenstown. Ph (03) 442-6082.

Toscana Italian Restaurant, 76 Golf Course Rd, Wanaka. Ph (03) 443-1255

The 19th Restaurant & Bar, Steamer Wharf, Queenstown. Ph (03) 442-4006.

OTAGO & SOUTHLAND

Totara Bar & Brasserie, Quality Hotel Brydone, 115 Thames St, Oamaru. Ph (03) 434-9892.

Bell Pepper Blues Restaurant, 474 Princes St, Dunedin. Ph (03) 474-0973.

Restaurant 95, 95 Filleul St, Dunedin. Ph (03) 471-9265.

2 Chefs Restaurant, 428 George St, Dunedin. Ph (03) 477-9117.

Donovan Restaurant, 220 Bainfield Rd, Invercargill. Ph (03) 215-8156.

Gazebo Restaurant & Bar, Croydon Lodge, Queenstown Highway, Gore. Ph (03) 208-9029.

Catlins Farmstay, 174 Progress Valley Rd, Southland. Ph (03) 246-8843.

Constable Cottage & Gaol, St Bathans, Central Otago. Ph (03) 447-3558.

Weights and Measures

For best results when you prepare the recipes, use standard metric measures (250ml cup, 15ml tablespoon and 5ml teaspoon) unless otherwise stated.*
Follow recipe instructions carefully, use level measurements and follow the specified cooking times. The oven temperature table opposite is a guide only. For best accuracy, refer to your own cooker instruction book.

*In NZ, USA and UK, 1 tablespoon = 15ml.
In Australia, 1 tablespoon = 20ml.

Oven Setting Equivalents (to nearest 10°C)

Description	Fahrenheit	Celsius	Gas Regulo No.
Very cool	225–275	110–140	1/4–1
Cool	300–325	150–160	2–3
Moderate	350–375	180–190	4–5
Hot	400–450	200–230	6–8
Very hot	475–500	250–260	9–10

Grams to Ounces: These are converted to the nearest round number.

Grams	Ounces	Grams	Ounces	Grams	Ounces
25	= 1	175	= 6	325	= 11
50	= 2	200	= 7	350	= 12
75	= 3	225	= 8	375	= 13
100	= 3.5	250	= 9	400	= 14
125	= 4	275	= 10	425	= 15
150	= 5	300	= 10.5	450	= 16

1 kilogram = 1000 grams = 2lb 4oz

Glossary

Arborio rice: a medium-grain Italian rice used in risotto (substitute with short-grain rice).

Béarnaise sauce: an egg-based sauce similar to Hollandaise with tarragon and chervil.

Beignet: choux pastry deep fried with sweet or savoury additions.

Bok choy: a Chinese green of the brassica family, with white stems and green tops. Best used when young and small. Substitute with spinach.

Bratwurst: normally a mildly spiced, precooked, pale sausage.

Cervena: a brand name for quality New Zealand venison.

Chorizo: a spicy, hot sausage.

Crème fraîche: cultured sour cream which does not separate on heating.

Enoki mushrooms: long stemmed with a tiny cap, available at Asian markets. Normally used for garnish.

Gelatine leaves: a stiff cellophane-like gelatine best used for fine textured jellies. Substitute with 1 teaspoon powdered gelatine to every 2 leaves.

Hijiki: thin, black, 'stringy' seaweed often used as a garnish after soaking.

Kaffir lime: also called makrut lime. Will grow leaves but no fruit normally in New Zealand. Fragrant leaves used in Thai food. Best used fresh or frozen rather than dried. If not available substitute with lime rind.

Mizuna: dark green feathery salad ingredient often seen in Mesclun salad mix, and can be stir-fried as well.

Nori: greenish/black seaweed sheet normally used in sushi.

Nougatine: a pale nutty caramel cut into shapes or moulded. Use praline if unavailable. (Praline is a thin toffee with toasted nuts in it which is ground up or crushed.)

Orzo: rice or barley-shaped pasta.

Pancetta: Italian. Pork belly, cured and sliced thinly. Substitute with prosciutto.

Panna Cotta: literally 'cooked cream' from Italy, usually sweetened and set with gelatine.

Pickled ginger: thin, pink slices of ginger in a brine, often used with sushi.

Pilaf: rice cooked with sautéed onion and stock or other flavourings.

Polenta: fine yellow cornmeal, often used as a porridge-like starch or cooled and fried.

Ponzu: a citrus/soy/fishy-flavoured sauce from Japan.

Prosciutto: airdried raw ham (Italian).

Quennelles: oval 'dumplings', but often the name is used to define the shape rather than the product. Chocolate mousse is an example. Shape with two dessert spoons.

Rainbow chard: a colourful variety of silverbeet/spinach.

Rocket: a slightly tangy salad green best eaten young. Can also be lightly cooked.

Scallopini: a small, round, green- or yellow-skinned squash like courgette, but with a nutty taste.

Scampi: a small crustacean, substitute with king prawns.

Shiitake mushroom: a delicately flavoured, slightly chewy mushroom, grown on wood.

Shoyu: light Japanese soy sauce, naturally fermented. Substitute with tamari.

Squid-ink linguini: black pasta flavoured and coloured with the 'ink' from squid.

Szechwan (sichuan, szechuan): peppercorns. A dried hot and spicy berry used in the province of the same name in China.

Tapenade: olive paste from Provence, usually with capers, anchovies, and olive oil.

Wasabi: Japanese horseradish usually sold as a ready-made paste or powder and used in sushi.

Wonton wrappers: small squares of noodle pastry.

Technical terms

Al dente: literally 'to the teeth' (Italian). When cooking pasta one should taste a bit towards the end of cooking time and there should be a little resistance as you bite.

Blind bake: when making a pastry base without a filling, baking paper or tinfoil is often weighted with rice or dry beans and placed on the pastry to keep it from puffing up while cooking in the early stages.

Char-grill: to sear at high heat on a ridged pan or barbecue or special char-grill element. This gives the familiar dark lines or patterns on steak or chicken or vegetables.

Dariole moulds: (usually metal) moulds in a small bucket shape used for individual desserts.

Deglaze: after frying, the pan is drained of fat and liquid (wine, stock, etc) is used to scrape up any pan-browned juices to add flavour to a sauce.

Julienne: small, fine, finger length strips (usually of vegetables).

Mirepoix: a fine dice usually of vegetables such as onion, carrot and celery.

Reduction: a liquid which is boiled hard to concentrate the flavour and reduce the quantity.

Refresh: to plunge into icy water after cooking to set the colour of vegetables.

'Sweat': to cook vegetables on a low heat in a little oil or butter without browning.

Recipe Index